The Tale of Audun of the West Fjords

Original Text, Translations, and Word Lists

Translated by
Matthew Leigh Embleton

Copyright ©2025 Matthew Leigh Embleton. All rights reserved.

The Tale of Audun of the West Fjords

The Tale of Auðun of the West Fjords (*Old Norse*) 4
Word List *(Old Norse to English)*..18
Word List *(English to Old Norse)* 27
The Tale of Auðun of the West Fjords (*Old Icelandic*)...34
Word List *(Old Icelandic to English)* 48
Word List *(English to Old Icelandic)* 57
A Word Comparison of Old Norse and Old Icelandic Words 64

Cover: Old Norse text over an outline of Iceland. Author's design.

The original Old Norse and Old Icelandic texts are in the public domain.
These translations ©2022 Matthew Leigh Embleton
©2025 Matthew Leigh Embleton (This Edition)

Acknowledgments

I have long been fascinated by languages and history, and I am very grateful to the special people in my life who have supported and encouraged me in my work. Thank you for believing in me. You know who you are.

Introduction

Old Norse is a North Germanic language spoken by inhabitants of Scandinavia from about the 7th to the 15th centuries. Old Icelandic is a variety of Old West Norse that emerged during the Norse settlement of Iceland in the second half of the 9th century. The rich tradition of Icelandic literature survived by oral tradition over several centuries before being written down in the 13th Century. The Tale of Auðun of the West Fjords (*Auðunar þáttr vestfirzka*) is one of the many Tales of Icelanders or *Íslendingaþættir*. The word '*þáttr*' (plural: '*þættir*') translates as a strand of rope or a yarn, comparable to the word 'yarn' in English sometimes used to refer to a story.

This book contains:
- The Tale of Auðun of the West Fjords (Auðunar þáttr vestfirzka) (Old Norse Version) from the Morkinskinna Book (GKS[1] 1009 fol., c. 1275, Royal Danish Library in Copenhagen)
- An Old Norse to English Word List
- An English to Old Norse Word List
- The Tale of Auðun of the West Fjords (Auðunar þáttur vestfirska) (Old Icelandic Version) from the Flateyjarbók (GkS 1005 fol., c. 1390, Árni Magnússon Institute for Icelandic Studies)
- An Old Icelandic to English Word List
- An English to Old Icelandic Word List
- A Word Comparison of Old Norse and Old Icelandic words

The texts are presented in their original form, with a literal word-for-word line-by-line translation, and a Modern English translation, all side-by-side. In this way, it is possible to see and feel how the worked and how it has evolved. This book is designed to be of use and interest to anyone with a passion for the Old Norse or Old Icelandic language, Norse history, or languages and history in general.

The Tale of Auðun of the West Fjords (Old Norse)

The Tale of Auðun of the West Fjords (*Old Norse*)

Auðunar þáttr vestfirzka, from the Morkinskinna Book (GKS[1] 1009 fol., c. 1275, Royal Danish Library in Copenhagen)

Old Norse	Literal	English
1	**1**	**1**
MAÐR hét Auðunn, vestfirzkr at kyni ok félítill.	Man named Audun, Westfjords by kin and fee-little.	There was a man named Audun, from the West Fjords by kin, and he was poor.
Hann fór útan vestr þar í fjörðum með umbráði Þorsteins, búanda góðs, ok Þóris stýrimanns, er þar hafði þegit vist of vetrinn með Þorsteini.	He travelled out west there in fields with managed Thorstein, farmer good, and Thorir skipper, who there had received hospitality over winter with Thorstein.	He travelled west to the fields which were managed by Thorstein, a good farmer, and Thorir who was a skipper, and they received hospitality from Thorstein over the winter.
Auðunn var ok þar ok starfaði fyrir honum Þóri ok þá þessi laun af honum, útanferðina ok hans umsjá.	Audun was also there and worked for him Thorir and then this reward of him, out-travelling and him about-see.	Audun was also there and worked for Thorir, and was rewarded by him with a place on his voyage, and taking care of him.
Hann Auðunn lagði mestan hluta fjár þess, er var, fyr móður sína, áðr hann stigi á skip, ok var kveðit á þriggja vetra björg.	He Audun laid most lot wealth this, that was, for mother his, after he climbed on the-ship, and was said of three winters aid.	Audun gave most of his wealth that was for his mother, once he had gone aboard the ship, and it was said to be three winters' worth of aid.
Ok nú fara þeir út heðan, ok ferst þeim vel, ok var Auðunn of vetrinn eftir með Þóri stýrimanni.	And now travelled they out hence, and travelled they well, and was Audun of winter afterwards with Thorir skipper.	And now they travelled out from there, and they travelled well, and Audun spent the winter afterwards with the skipper Thorir.
Hann átti bú á Mæri.	He had a-farm in Moer.	He had a farm in Moer.
Ok um sumarit eftir fara þeir út til Grænlands ok eru þar of vetrinn.	And about summer afterwards travelled they out to Greenland and were there of winter.	And around the summer afterwards they travelled out to Greenland and were there for the winter.
Þess er við getit, at Auðunn kaupir þar bjarndýri eitt, gersimi mikla, ok gaf þar fyrir alla eigu sína.	This is with told-of, that Audun bought there a-bear one, treasured much, and gave there for all owned his.	It is told that Audun bought a bear there, which was much treasured, and gave all that he owned for it.

The Tale of Auðun of the West Fjords (Old Norse)

Old Norse	Literal	English
Ok nú of sumarit eftir þá fara þeir aftr til Nóregs ok verða vel reiðfara.	And now of summer afterwards then travelled they returning to Norway and was well voyage.	And now about the summer afterwards then they travelled returning to Norway and the voyage went well.
Hefir Auðunn dýr sitt með sér ok ætlar nú at fara suðr til Danmerkr á fund Sveins konungs ok gefa honum dýrit.	Had Audun wild-animal his with him and intended now to travel south to Denmark to meet Svein the-king and give him the-beast.	Audun had his wild-animal with him and intended now to travel south to Denmark to meet King Svein and give him the beast.
Ok er hann kom suðr í landit, þar sem konungr var fyrir, þá gengr hann upp af skipi ok leiðir eftir sér dýrit ok leigir sér herbergi.	And as he came south to land, there as the-king was present, then went he up off the-ship and took behind him the-beast and rented himself a-room.	And as he came south to land, where the king was present, he then went up off the ship and took the beast with him and rented himself a room.
Haraldi konungi var sagt brátt, at þar var komit bjarndýri, gersimi mikil, ok á íslenzkr maðr.	Harald the-king was told soon, that there was come a-bear, treasured much, and an Icelander man.	King Harald was soon told, that a bear had come, which was much treasured, and an Icelander.
Konungr sendir þegar menn eftir honum,	The-king sent straight-away people after him,	The king sent people to fetch him straight away,
ok er Auðunn kom fyrir konung, kveðr hann konung vel.	and as Audun came before the-king, greeted he the-king well.	and when Audun came before the king, he greeted the king well.
Konungr tók vel kveðju hans ok spurði síðan:	The-king took well greeting his and asked afterwards:	The king received his greeting well and afterwards asked:
"Áttu gersimi mikla í bjarndýri?"	"Have-you treasured much a bear?"	"Do you have a bear which is much treasured?".
Hann svarar ok kveðst eiga dýrit eitthvert.	He answered and said owned a-beast some-kind.	He answered and said that he owned a beast of some kind.
Konungr mælti:	The-king spoke:	The king spoke:
"Villtu selja oss dýrit við slíku verði sem þú keyptir?"	"Will-you sell us the-beast with such worth as you bought?"	"Will you sell us the beast for the same worth as you bought it?".
Hann svarar:	He answered:	He answered:
"Eigi vil ek þat, herra?"	"Not wish I that, lord?"	"I do not wish to do that, lord".

The Tale of Auðun of the West Fjords (Old Norse)

Old Norse	Literal	English
"Villtu þá", segir konungr, "at ek gefa þér tvau verð slík, ok mun þat réttara, ef þú hefir þar við gefit alla þína eigu?"	"Will-you then", said the-king, "that I give to-you twice worth such, and should that righter, if you have there with given all you own?"	"Do you wish then", said the king, "that I give you twice the worth, and that should be right, if you have given all you own for it?".
"Eigi vil ek þat, herra", segir hann.	"Not wish I that, lord", said he.	"I do not wish to do that, lord", he said.
Konungr mælti:	The-king spoke:	The king spoke:
"Villtu gefa mér þá?"	"Will-you give me then?"	"Will you give it to me then?".
Hann svarar:	He answered:	He answered:
"Eigi, herra".	"Not lord".	"I will not, lord".
Konungr mælti:	The-king spoke:	The king spoke:
"Hvat villtu þá af gera?"	"What will-you then of do?"	"What do you wish to do then?".
Hann svarar:	He answered:	He answered:
"Fara", segir hann, "til Danmerkr ok gefa Sveini konungi".	Travel", said he, "to Denmark and give Svein the-king".	"Travel", said he, to Denmark and give it to King Svein".
Haraldr konungr segir:	Harald the-king said:	King Harald said:
"Hvárt er, at þú ert maðr svá óvitr, at þú hefir eigi heyrt ófrið þann, er í milli er landa þessa, eða ætlar þú giftu þína svá mikla, at þú munir þar komast með gersimar, er aðrir fá eigi komizt klaklaust, þó at nauðsyn eigi til?"	"Whether is, that you are a-man so unwise, that you have none heard un-peace then, that is between the land this, or suppose you gift yours so much, that you would there come with treasure, that others get none coming unhurt, though that necessary not to?"	"Is it possible, that you are an unwise man, that you have not heard of the state of war that is between these lands, or you suppose that you are so gifted that you would come there with treasure, where others have not gone unhurt though it was necessary?".
Auðunn svarar:	Audun answered:	Audun answered:
"Herra, þat er á yðru valdi, en engu játum vér öðru en þessu, er vér höfum áðr ætlat".	"Lord that is for your will, but none profess we other than this, that we have before intended".	"That is for your will lord, but I cannot agree to anything other than what I have previously intended".
Þá mælti konungr:	Then spoke the-king:	Then the king spoke:

The Tale of Auðun of the West Fjords (Old Norse)

Old Norse	Literal	English
"Hví mun eigi þat til, at þú farir leið þína, sem þú vill, ok kom þá til mín, er þú ferr aftr, ok seg mér, hversu Sveinn konungr launar þér dýrit, ok kann þat vera, at þú sér gæfumaðr".	"Why should not that to, that you travel journey yours, as you wish, and come then to me, when you travel back, and say to-me, how-so Svein the-king repays your beast, and can that be, that you yourself gifted-man".	"Then why should you not, to travel on your journey, as you wish, and then come to me, when you travel back, and tell me how King Svein repays you for the beast, and can it be, that you will be a gifted man".
"Því heit ek þér", sagði Auðunn.	"Accordingly promise I to-you", said Audun.	"I promise this to you accordingly", said Audun.
Hann ferr nú síðan suðr með landi ok í Vík austr ok þá til Danmerkr, ok er þá uppi hverr penningr fjárins, ok verðr hann þá biðja matar bæði fyr sik ok fyr dýrit.	He travelled now afterwards south along land and to Vik east and then to Denmark, and was then up every penny of-wealth, and was he then begging food both for himself and for the-beast.	He now travelled afterwards south along the land and to Vik east and then to Denmark, and then every penny of his wealth was spent, and he was then begging for food both for himself and for the beast.
Hann kemr á fund ármanns Sveins konungs, þess er Áki hét, ok bað hann vista nökkurra bæði fyr sik ok fyr dýrit,	He came to meet steward Svein's the-king, this was Aki named, and asked him provisions some asked for himself and for the-beast,	He came to meet a steward of King Svein, who was named Aki, and he asked him for some provisions for himself and for the beast,
"ek ætla", segir hann, "at gefa Sveini konungi dýrit".	"I intend", said he, "to give Svein the-king the-beast".	I intend, he said, "to give this beast to King Svein".
Áki lézt selja mundu honum vistir, ef hann vildi.	Aki said sell would him provisions, if he wished.	Aki said that he would sell him provisions if he wished.
Auðunn kveðst ekki til hafa fyrir at gefa, "en ek vilda þó", segir hann, "at þetta kæmist til leiðar, at ek mætta dýrit færa konungi".	Audun said not to have for to give, "and I wish though", said he, "that this comes to the-way, that I might the-beast bring the-king".	Audun said that he did not have anything to give, "and though I wish", he said, "that I may be able t bring this beast to the king".
"Ek mun fá þér vistir, sem þit þurfuð til konungs fundar, en þar í móti vil ek eiga hálft dýrit, ok máttu á þat líta, at dýrit mun deyja fyrir þér, þars þit þurfuð vistir miklar, en fé sé farit, ok er búit við, at þú hafir þá ekki dýrsins".	"I shall give you provisions, that you need to the-king meet, then there on meeting will I own half the-beast, and might be that look, that the-beast could die for you, there you need provisions much, but money is gone, and is settled with, that you have then not the-beast".	"I shall give you provisions, that you need to meet the king, then on meeting him I will own half the beast, otherwise it might be, that the beast could die before you, there you will need many provisions, but your money is gone, and it shall be that you will then not have the beast".

The Tale of Auðun of the West Fjords (Old Norse)

Old Norse	Literal	English
Ok er hann lítr á þetta, sýnist honum nökkut eftir sem ármaðrinn mælti fyrir honum, ok sættast þeir á þetta, at hann selr Áka hálft dýrit, ok skal konungr síðan meta allt saman.	And when he looked a this, considered he sometime afterwards what steward spoke before him, and reconciled they to this, that he sell Aki half the-beast, and shall the-king afterwards value all the-same.	And when he looked at this, he considered for some time afterwards what the steward had said to him, and they reconciled to this, that he would sell Aki half of the beast, and the king would afterwards value it all the same.
Skulu þeir fara báðir nú á fund konungs, ok svá gera þeir, fara nú báðir á fund konungs ok stóðu fyr borðinu.	Shall they travel both now and meet the-king, and so did they, travelled now both to meet the-king and stood before table.	And should they now both travel and meet the king, and they did so, they both travelled to meet the king and stood before his tables.
Konungr íhugaði, hverr þessi maðr myndi vera, er hann kenndi eigi, ok mælti síðan til Auðunar:	The-king considered, who this man should be, that he knew not, and spoke then to Audun:	The king considered, who this man should be, that he did not know, and then spoke to Audun:
"Hverr ertu?" segir hann.	"Who are-you?" said he.	"Who are you?" he said.
Hann svarar:	He answered:	He answered:
"Ek em íslenzkr maðr, herra", segir hann, "ok kominn nú útan af Grænlandi ok nú af Nóregi, ok ætlaðak at færa yðr bjarndýr þetta.	"I am Icelander man, lord", said he, "and coming now out out-of Greenland and now from Norway, and intended to bring your bear this.	"I am an Icelander, lord", he said, "and I have come from Greenland and from Norway intending to bring you this bear.
Keyptak þat með allri eigu minni, ok nú er þó á orðit mikit fyrir mér, ek á nú hálft eitt dýrit", ok segir konungi síðan, hversu farit hafði með þeim Áka, ármanni hans.	Purchased that with all own mine, and now is though that become much for me, I of not half one beast", and told-the-king then, how-so fared had with them Aki, the-steward his.	I purchased it with all that I own, and now though it has become much for me, I do not own half of the beast", and he then told the king, how it had gone with Aki, his steward.
Konungr mælti:	The-king spoke:	The king spoke:
"Er þat satt, Áki, er hann segir?"	"Is that true, Aki, what he says?"	"Is that true, Aki, what he says?".
"Satt er þat", segir hann.	"True is that", said he.	"That is true", he said.
Konungr mælti:	The-king spoke:	The king spoke:

The Tale of Auðun of the West Fjords (Old Norse)

Old Norse	Literal	English
"Ok þótti þér þat til liggja, þar sem ek settak þik mikinn mann, at hefta þat eða tálma, er maðr gerðist til at færa mér gersimi ok gaf fyrir alla eign ok sá þat Haraldr konungr at ráði at láta hann fara í friði, ok er hann várr óvinr?	"And thought you that to lay-out, then since I intended you a-great man, to stop that or prevent, as a-man did to that bring to-me treasure and gave because all owned and so that Harald the-king that decided to let him travel in peace, and that he our un-friend	"And you thought to let this happen, even though I intended you to be a great man, to stop or prevent, as a man made to bring this treasure and give to me all that he owned, and even though King Harald decided to let him travel in peace, even though he is our enemy?
Hygg þú at þá, hvé sannligt þat var þinnar handar, ok þat væri makligt, at þú værir drepinn.	Think you that then, how true-like that was your hand, and that should-be proper, that you would-be killed.	Think then how true your hand was, and it would be right, that you should be killed.
En ek mun nú eigi þat gera, en braut skaltu fara þegar ór landinu ok koma aldrigi aftr síðan mér í augsýn.	But I should now not that do, but away shall travel straight-away out-of this-land and come never back after to-me in eyesight.	I will not do what I should, but you shall travel away immediately out of this land and never come back in my sight.
En þér, Auðunn, kann ek slíka þökk sem þú gefir mér allt dýrit, ok ver hér með mér".	But you, Audun, can I such thanks as you gave me all animal, and be here with me".	But you, Audun, can I thank such as you gave me the whole animal, and be here with me".
Þat þekkist hann ok er með Sveini konungi um hríð.	That knew he and was with Svein the-king about awhile.	That he knew, and he was with King Svein for a while.

2

Ok er liðu nökkurar stundir, þá mælti Auðunn við konung:	And as passed some time, then spoke Audun with the-king:	And as some time has passed, then Audun spoke with the king:
"Braut fýsir mik nú, herra".	"Away desire me now, lord".	"I desire now to travel away, lord".
Konungr svarar heldr seint:	The-king answered rather coldly:	The king answered rather coldly:
"Hvat villtu þá", segir hann, "ef þú vill eigi með oss vera?"	"What will-you then", said he, "if you wish not with us be?"	"What do you wish for then", he said, "if not to be with us?".
Hann segir:	He said:	He said:

The Tale of Auðun of the West Fjords (Old Norse)

Old Norse	Literal	English
"Suðr vil ek ganga".	"South wish I to-go".	"I wish to go south".
"Ef þú vildir eigi svá gott ráð taka", segir konungr, "þá myndi mér fyr þykkja í, er þú fýsist í brott".	"If you wish not so good course take", said the-king, "then would me for think it, that you desire to away".	"If you did not wish to take such a good course", said the king, "I would mind it to think that you desire to go away".
Ok nú gaf konungr honum silfr mjök mikit, ok fór hann suðr síðan með Rúmferlum, ok skipaði konungr til um ferð hans, bað hann koma til sín, er hann kæmi aftr.	And now gave the-king him silver much great, and travelled he south afterwards with Rome-travellers, and directed the-king to about travel his, asked him come to him, when he came returning.	And now the king gave him much great silver, and he travelled south afterwards with pilgrims, and the king made arrangements for his journey, and asked him to come to him when he returned.
Nú fór hann ferðar sinnar, unz hann kemr suðr í Rómaborg.	Now travelled he journey his, until he came south to Rome-city.	Now he travelled on his journey, until he came south to Rome.
Ok er hann hefir þar dvalizt, sem hann tíðir, þá ferr hann aftr, tekr þá sótt mikla, gerir hann þá ákafliga magran.	And when he had there dwelled, such he a-time, then travelled he returning, took then sickness much, made him then extremely thin.	And when he had dwelled there for such a time, he travelled to return, and took to much sickness, which made him extremely thin.
Gengr þá upp allt féit, þat er konungr hafði gefit honum til ferðarinnar, tekr síðan upp stafkarlsstíg ok biðr sér matar.	Went then up all treasure, that which the-king had given him to travelling, taking afterwards up begging and asked he food.	Gone was all his treasure, which the king had given him for travelling, and afterwards he took to begging and he asked for food.
Hann er þá kollóttr ok heldr ósælligr.	He was then bald and rather unhappy.	He was then bald and rather unhappy.
Hann kemr aftr í Danmörk at páskum, þangat sem konungr er þá staddr, en eigi þorði hann at láta sjá sik ok var í kirkjuskoti ok ætlaði þá til fundar við konung, er hann gengi til kirkju um kveldit.	He came back to Denmark at Easter, there as the-king was then standing, but not dared he to let seen himself and was in church-wing and intended then to meet with the-king, when he went to church around evening.	He came back to Denmark at Easter, there where the king was standing, but he dared not to let himself be seen, and was in the church wing and intended to meet with the king, when he went to church in the evening.
Ok nú er hann sá konunginn ok hirðina fagrliga búna, þá þorði hann eigi at láta sjá sik.	And now when he saw the-king and guardsmen beautifully prepared, then dared he not to let seen himself.	And now when he saw the king and the guardsmen so beautifully dressed, then he dared not to let himself be seen.

The Tale of Auðun of the West Fjords (Old Norse)

Old Norse	Literal	English
Ok er konungr gekk til drykkju í höllina, þá mataðist Auðunn úti, sem siðr er til Rúmferla, meðan þeir hafa eigi kastat staf ok skreppu.	And when the-king went to drinking in the-hall, then ate Audun outside, as custom is for Rome-travellers, while they have not cast staff and pouch.	And when the king went drinking in the hall, Audun ate outside, which was the custom for pilgrims, while they have cast aside their staff and pouch.
Ok nú of aftaninn, er konungr gekk til kveldsöngs, ætlaði Auðunn at hitta hann, ok svá mikit sem honum þótti fyrr fyr, jók nú miklu á, er þeir váru drukknir hirðmenninir.	And now of evening, as the-king going to evensong, intended Audun to meet him, and so much as he thought for before, increased now much for, that they were in-drink the-courtiers.	And now in the evening, as the king was going to evensong, Audun intended to meet him, and as much as he had thought before was now increased, because the courtiers were drunk.
Ok er þeir gengu inn aftr, þá þekði konungr mann ok þóttist finna, at eigi hafði frama til at ganga fram at hitta hann.	And as they went inside back, then noticed the-king a-man and thought found, that not had confidence to that going from to meet him.	And as they went back inside, then the king thought he noticed a man thought he found, that he did not have the confidence in going to meet him.
Ok nú er hirðin gekk inn, þá veik konungr út ok mælti:	And now as the-courtiers going inside, then turned-to the-king out and spoke:	And now as the courtiers were going inside, then the king turned and spoke out:
"Gangi sá nú fram, er mik vill finna.	"Come so now forth, who me wishes to-meet.	"Come forth now, who wishes to meet me.
Mik grunar, at sá muni vera maðrinn".	I suspect, that so shall be a-man".	For I suspect that there is such a man".
Þá gekk Auðunn fram ok fell til fóta konungi, ok varla kenndi konungr hann.	Then went Audun forth and fell to feet the-king's, and hardly recognised the-king him.	Then Audun went forth and fell at the king's feet, and the king hardly recognised him.
Ok þegar er konungr veit, hverr hann er, tók konungr í hönd honum Auðuni ok bað hann vel kominn, "ok hefir þú mikit skipazt", segir hann, "síðan vit sáumst", leiðir hann eftir sér inn.	And as-soon-as that the-king knew, who he was, took the-king in hand him Audun and bid him well come, "and have you much changed", said he, "since we saw", led he after him inside.	And as soon as the king knew who he was, the king took Audun in hand and bid him welcome, "and you have changed much", he said, "since we last saw each other", and after he led him inside.
Ok er hirðin sá hann, hlógu þeir at honum, en konungr sagði:	And when courtiers saw him, laughed they at him, but the-king said:	And when the courtiers saw him, they laughed at him, but the king said:

The Tale of Auðun of the West Fjords (Old Norse)

Old Norse	Literal	English
"Eigi þurfuð þér at honum at hlæja, því at betr hefir hann sét fyrir sinni sál heldr en þér".	"None need you that him to laugh, because that better has he himself seen for his soul rather than you".	"None of you need to laugh at him, because he has seen better for his soul than any of you".
Þá lét konungr gera honum laug ok gaf honum síðan klæði, ok er hann nú með honum.	Then had the-king made him bath and gave him afterwards clothes, and was he now with him.	Then the king had a bath made for him, and afterwards gave him clothes, and he was now with him.

3

Old Norse	Literal	English
Þat er nú sagt, einhverju sinni of várit, at konungr býðr Auðuni at vera með sér álengðar ok kveðst mundu gera hann skutilsvein sinn ok leggja til hans góða virðing.	It is now said, one-such on-the-way to spring, that the-king bid Audun to be with him all-longer and said would make him cup-bearer his and grant to him good worth.	It is now said, that on the way to spring, the king invited Audun to be with him for all of his days, and said that he would make him his cup-bearer and grant him good worthiness.
Auðunn segir:	Audun said:	Audun said:
"Guð þakki yðr, herra, sóma þann allan, er þér vilið til mín leggja, en hitt er mér í skapi, at fara út til Íslands".	"God thank you, lord, honour this all, that you wish to me grant, but find I to-me of mind, to travel out to Iceland".	"God thank you, lord, for all this honour that you wish to grant me, but I find in my mind, to travel out to Iceland".
Konungr segir:	The-king said:	The king said:
"Þetta sýnist mér undarliga kosit".	"This seems to-me strange choice".	"This seems a strange choice to me".
Auðunn mælti:	Audun spoke:	Audun spoke:
"Eigi má ek þat vita, herra", segir hann, "at ek hafa hér mikinn sóma með yðr, en móðir mín troði stafkarls stíg út á Íslandi, því at nú er lokit björg þeiri, er ek lagða til, áðr ek færa af Íslandi".	"Not may I that know, lord", said he, "that I have here much honour with you, but mother mine treads the-beggar's path out in Iceland, for that now is ended help there, that I enriched to, before I travelled from Iceland".	"Not may I know, lord", said he, "that I have much honour here with you, but my mother treads the beggar's path out in Iceland, for now my help there is ended, that which I enriched her with, before I travelled out from Iceland".
Konungr svarar:	The-king answered:	The king answered:
"Vel er mælt", segir hann, "ok mannliga, ok muntu verða giftumaðr.	"Well is spoken", said he, "and man-like, and shall-you be gifted-man.	"It is well spoken", said he, "and like a man, and you shall be a gifted man.

The Tale of Auðun of the West Fjords (Old Norse)

Old Norse	Literal	English
Sjá einn var svá hlutrinn, at mér myndi eigi mislíka, at þú færir í braut heðan, ok ver nú með mér, þar til er skip búast".	So one as such thing, that to-me should not mislike, that you travel to away from-here, and be now with me, then until that ship prepared".	So there is one such thing, that I should not dislike, that you travel away from here, and be now with me, then until a ship is prepared".
Hann gerir svá.	He did so.	He did so.
Einn dag, er á leið várit, gekk Sveinn konungr ofan á bryggjur, ok váru menn þá at at búa skip til ýmissa landa, í Austrveg eða Saxland, til Svíþjóðar eða Nóregs.	One day, when it passed spring, went Svein the-king over-to the quay, and were people then about that prepared ships to various lands, in Eastern-lands or Saxon-lands, to Sweden or Norway.	One day, when spring had passed, King Svein went over to the quay, and there were people about preparing ships for various lands, Eastern-lands, Saxon-lands, to Sweden or Norway.
Þá koma þeir Auðunn at einu skipi fögru, ok váru menn at at búa skipit.	Then came there Audun to one ship beautiful, and were people that it prepared ship.	Then Audun came to a beautiful ship, and there were people that were preparing the ship.
Þá spurði konungr:	Then asked the-king:	Then the king asked:
"Hversu lízt þér, Auðunn, á þetta skip?"	"How-so appears to-you, Audun, about this ship?"	"How does this ship appear to you, Audun?"
Hann svarar:	He answered:	He answered:
"Vel, herra".	"Well lord".	"Well lord".
Konungr mælti:	The-king spoke:	The king spoke:
"Þetta skip vil ek þér gefa ok launa bjarndýrit".	"This ship wish I to-you give and reward the-bear".	"I wish to give you this ship as a reward for the bear".
Hann þakkaði gjöfina eftir sinni kunnustu.	He thanked the-gift after he knew-how.	He thanked him for the gift as well as he knew how.
Ok er leið stund ok skipit var albúit, þá mælti Sveinn konungr við Auðun:	And when passed awhile and ship was all-prepared, then spoke Svein the-king with Audun:	And when a while had passed and the ship was all prepared, then King Svein spoke with Audun:

The Tale of Auðun of the West Fjords (Old Norse)

Old Norse	Literal	English
"Þó villtu nú á braut, þá mun ek nú ekki letja þik, en þat hefi ek spurt, at illt er til hafna fyrir landi yðru, ok eru víða öræfi ok hætt skipum.	"Though will now to away, then should I now not discourage you, but it have I heard, that ill is to harbour for land yours, and they-are widely wild and at-risk ships.	"Though you now wish to go away, then I should not now discourage you, but I have heard that bad are the harbours in your land, and they are widely wild and ships are at risk.
Nú brýtr þú ok týnir skipinu ok fénu.	Now wrecked you and lose the-ship and cargo.	Now should your ship be wrecked and you lose your ship and cargo.
Lítt sér þat þá á, at þú hafir fundit Svein konung ok gefit honum gersimi".	Little to-you that then be, that you have met Svein the-king and gave him treasure".	You shall have little to say that you have met King Svein and gave him treasure".
Síðan seldi konungr honum leðrhosu fulla af silfri, "ok ertu þá enn eigi félauss með öllu, þótt þú brjótir skipit, ef þú fær haldit þessu.	Afterwards handed-over the-king to-him leather-purse full of silver, "and are-you then one not money-less with all, though you wrecked ship, if you go holding this.	Afterwards the king handed over to him a leather purse full of silver, "and are you then not penniless, even though your ship is wrecked, if you hold on to this.
Verða má svá enn", segir konungr, "at þú týnir þessu fé. Lítt nýtr þú þá þess, er þú fannt Svein konung ok gaft honum gersimi".	Become may so then", said the-king, "that you lose this money. Little benefit you then this, that you found Svein the-king and gave him treasure".	But if it becomes then", said the king, "that you lose this money. It will benefit you little then, that you have met King Svein and given him treasure".
Síðan dró konungr hring af hendi sér ok gaf Auðuni ok mælti:	Then drew the-king a-ring of hand his and gave Audun and spoke:	Then the king drew a ring from his hand and gave it to Audun saying:
"Þó at svá illa verði, at þú brjótir skipit ok týnir fénu, eigi ertu félauss, ef þú kemst á land, því at margir menn hafa gull á sér í skipsbrotum, ok sér þá, at þú hefir fundit Svein konung, ef þú heldr hringinum.	"Though that so ill be, that you wrecked ship and lose money, not are-you money-less, if you came to land, therefore that many people have gold about themselves for ship-wreck, and yourself then, that you have met Svein the-king, if you hold the-ring.	"Even though it would be so bad if your ship was wrecked, and you lose all the money, you shall not be penniless, therefore many people have gold about themselves in case of being shipwrecked, and you shall have met King Svein, if you hold on to this ring.

The Tale of Auðun of the West Fjords (Old Norse)

Old Norse	Literal	English
En þat vil ek ráða þér", segir hann, "at þú gefir eigi hringinn, nema þú þykkist eiga svá mikit gott at launa nökkurum göfgum manni, þá gef þeim hringinn, því at tígnum mönnum sómir at þiggja.	But that wish I advise to-you", said he, "that you give not the-ring, except you think not so much good to reward some noble man, then give them the-ring, for that dignified people honourable that accept.	But I wish to advise you", he said, "that you do not give the ring to anyone, unless you think it will be good to reward some noble man, then give them the ring, for dignified and honourable people will accept.
Ok far nú heill".	And travel now whole".	And now travel whole".

4

Old Norse	Literal	English
Síðan lætr hann í haf ok kemr í Nóreg ok lætr flytja upp varnað sinn, ok þurfti nú meira við þat en fyrr, er hann var í Nóregi.	Afterwards laid he to sea and came to Norway and had carried up wares his, and needed now more with that than before, when he was in Norway.	Afterwards he put to sea and came to Norway and had his wares carried up, which he needed more now than before, when he was in Norway.
Hann ferr nú síðan á fund Haralds konungs ok vill efna þat, er hann hét honum, áðr hann fór til Danmerkr, ok kveðr konung vel.	He travelled not afterwards to meet Harald the-king and wished carry-out that, which he promised him, before he travelled to Denmark, and greeted the-king well.	He travelled now afterwards to meet King Harald, as he wished to carry out what he had promised him, before he travelled to Denmark, and he greeted the king well.
Haraldr konungr tók vel kveðju hans, "ok sezt niðr", segir hann, "ok drekk hér með oss".	Harald the-king received well greeting his, "and sit down", said he, "and drink here with us".	King Harald received his greeting well, "and sit down", he said, "and drink here with us".
Ok svá gerir hann.	And so did he.	And so he did.
Þá spurði Haraldr konungr:	Then asked Harald the-king:	Then King Harald asked:
"Hverju launaði Sveinn konungr þér dýrit?"	"How rewarded Svein the-king you the-beast?"	"How did King Svein reward you for the beast?".
Auðunn svarar:	Audun answered:	Audun answered:
"Því, herra, at hann þá at mér".	"Because lord, that he then at me".	"Because lord, that he accepted it of me".
Konungr sagði:	The-king said:	The king said:

The Tale of Auðun of the West Fjords (Old Norse)

Old Norse	Literal	English
"Launat mynda ek þér því hafa. Hverju launaði hann enn?"	"Repaid would I you accordingly have. How rewarded he then?"	"I would have repaid you accordingly. How did he reward you then?".
Auðunn svarar:	Audun answered:	Audun answered:
"Gaf hann mér silfr til suðrgöngu".	"Gave he me silver to south-going".	"He gave me silver to go south".
Þá segir Haraldr konungr:	Then said Harald the-king:	Then King Harald said:
"Mörgum manni gefr Sveinn konungr silfr til suðrgöngu eða annarra hluta, þótt ekki færi honum gersimar.	"Many people gives Svein the-king silver to south-going or others lots, though not bring him treasure.	"King Svein gives many people silver to go south, lots of others, though they do not bring him treasure".
Hvat er enn fleira?"	What was it more?"	What was it more?".
"Hann bauð mér", segir Auðunn, "at gerast skutilsveinn hans ok mikinn sóma til mín at leggja".	"He bid me", said Audun, "to be cup-bearer his and much honour to me that granted".	"He invited me", said Audun, "to be his cup-bearer and to grant me much honour".
"Vel var þat mælt", segir konungr, "ok launa myndi hann enn fleira".	"Well was that said", said the-king, "and rewarded would he then more".	"That was well said", said the king, "and he would reward you more".
Auðunn segir:	Audun said:	Audun said:
"Gaf hann mér knörr með farmi þeim, er hingat er bezt varit í Nóreg".	"Gave he me a-ship with cargo then, that there was best wares in Norway".	"He then gave me a ship with cargo, of wares that sell best in Norway".
"Þat var stórmannligt", segir konungr, "en launat mynda ek þér því hafa. Launaði hann því fleira?"	"That was great-man-like", said the-king, "but rewarded would I you accordingly have. Rewarded he then more?"	"That was generous", said the king, "but I would have rewarded you accordingly. Did he reward you then more?".
Auðunn segir:	Audun said:	Audun said:
"Gaf hann mér leðrhosu fulla af silfri ok kvað mik þá eigi félausan, ef ek helda því, þó at skip mitt bryti við Ísland".	"Gave he to-me leather-purse full of silver and said to-me then not money-less, if I held therefore, though that ship mine break at Iceland".	"He gave me a leather purse full of silver, and said to me that if I held it I would therefore not be penniless, even if my ship was wrecked in Iceland".
Konungr segir:	The-king said:	The king said:

The Tale of Auðun of the West Fjords (Old Norse)

Old Norse	Literal	English
"Þat var ágætliga gert, ok þat mynda ek ekki gert hafa. Lauss mynda ek þykkjast, ef ek gæfa þér skipit. Hvárt launaði hann fleira?"	"That was greatly done, and that would I not done have. Less should I seem, if I gave you the-ship. How rewarded he more?"	"That was greatly done, and I would not have done that. Less would I think, if I gave you the ship. How did he reward you more?".
"Svá var víst, herra", segir Auðunn, "at hann launaði. Hann gaf mér hring þenna, er ek hefi á hendi, ok kvað svá mega at berast, at ek týnda fénu öllu, ok sagði mik þá eigi félausan, ef ek ætta hringinn, ok bað mik eigi lóga, nema ek ætta nökkurum tígnum manni svá gott at launa, at ek vilda gefa.	"So was certainly, lord", said Audun, "that he rewarded. He gave me ring this, that I have in hand, and said so may it bear, that I lose money all, and said to-me then not money-less, if I had the-ring, and bid me not lose, except I have some noble man so good to repay, that I wish give.	"So it certainly was, lord", said Audun, "that he rewarded. He gave me this ring, that I have in hand, and so it may bear, though I lose all my money, it is said to me that I would not be penniless, if I had the ring, and he asked me not to part with it, unless I have some noble man so good to repay, that I wish to give it to.
En nú hefi ek þann fundit, því at þú áttir kost at taka hvárttveggja frá mér, dýrit ok svá líf mitt, en þú lézt mik fara þangat í friði, sem aðrir náðu eigi".	But now have I then found, because that you have benefit to take either-way from me, the-beast and so life mine, but you let me travel from-here in peace, as others reached not".	But now then I have found, because you could have taken away from me, the beast or my life, but you let me travel from here in peace, as others could not".
Konungr tók við gjöfinni með blíðu ok gaf Auðuni í móti góðar gjafar, áðr en þeir skildist.	The-king received with the-gift with joyfulness and gave Audun in return good gifts, before that they separated.	The king received the gift with joyfulness and gave Audun good gifts in return, before they separated.
Auðunn varði fénu til Íslandsferðar ok fór út þegar um sumarit til Íslands ok þótti vera inn mesti gæfumaðr.	Audun was wealth to Iceland-journey and travelled out from-there about summer to Iceland and thought was the most gifted-man.	Audun used his wealth to travel to Iceland and travelled out from there around summer to Iceland and he was thought of as the most gifted man.
Frá þessum manni, Auðuni, var kominn Þorsteinn Gyðuson.	From this people, Audun, was descended Thorstein Gyduson.	From these people, Audun, were descended Thorstein Gyduson.

Word List *(Old Norse to English)*

Old Norse	English

A, a

aðrir	others
af	from, of, off, out-of
aftaninn	evening
aftr	back, returning
albúit	all-prepared
aldrigi	never
alla	all
allan	all
allri	all
allt	all
annarra	others
at	about, at, by, it, that, to
Auðun	Audun (name)
Auðunar	Audun (name)
Auðuni	Audun (name)
Auðunn	Audun (name)
augsýn	eyesight
austr	east
Austrveg	Eastern-lands (place)

Á, á

á	a, about, an, and, be, for, in, it, of, on, that, the, to
áðr	after, before
ágætliga	greatly
Áka	Aki (name)
ákafliga	extremely
Áki	Aki (name)
álengðar	all-longer
ármaðrinn	steward
ármanni	the-steward
ármanns	steward
átti	had
áttir	have
áttu	have-you

Æ, æ

ætla	intend
ætlaðak	intended
ætlaði	intended
ætlar	intend, intended
ætlat	intended
ætta	had, have

B, b

bað	asked, bid
báðir	both
bæði	asked, both
bauð	bid
berast	bear
betr	better
bezt	best
biðja	begging
biðr	asked
bjarndýr	bear
bjarndýri	a-bear, bear
bjarndýrit	the-bear
björg	aid, help
blíðu	joyfulness
borðinu	table
brátt	soon
braut	away
brjótir	wrecked
brott	away
bryggjur	quay
bryti	break
brýtr	wrecked
bú	a-farm
búa	prepared
búanda	farmer
búast	prepared
búit	settled
búna	prepared
býðr	bid

Word List (Old Norse to English)

Old Norse	English

D, d

dag	day
Danmerkr	Denmark (place)
Danmörk	Denmark (place)
deyja	die
drekk	drink
drepinn	killed
dró	drew
drukknir	in-drink
drykkju	drinking
dvalizt	dwelled
dýr	wild-animal
dýrit	a-beast, animal, beast, the-beast
dýrsins	the-beast

E, e

eða	or
ef	if
efna	carry-out
eftir	after, afterwards, behind
eiga	not, own, owned
eigi	none, not
eign	owned
eigu	own, owned
einhverju	one-such
einn	one
einu	one
eitt	one
eitthvert	some-kind
ek	I
ekki	not
em	am
en	and, but, than, that, then
engu	none
enn	it, one, then
er	as, I, is, that, the, was, what, when, which, who
ert	are
ertu	are-you
eru	they-are, were

F, f

fá	get, give
fær	go
færa	bring, travelled
færi	bring
færir	travel
fagrliga	beautifully
fannt	found
far	travel
fara	travel, travelled
farir	travel
farit	fared, gone
farmi	cargo
fé	money
féit	treasure
félausan	money-less
félauss	money-less
félítill	fee-little
fell	fell
fénu	cargo, money, wealth
ferð	travel
ferðar	journey
ferðarinnar	travelling
ferr	travel, travelled
ferst	travelled
finna	found, to-meet
fjár	wealth
fjárins	of-wealth
fjörðum	fields
fleira	more
flytja	carried
fögru	beautiful
fór	travelled
fóta	feet
frá	from
fram	forth, from
frama	confidence
friði	peace
fulla	full
fund	meet
fundar	meet
fundit	found, met
fyr	before, for

Word List (Old Norse to English)

Old Norse	English
fyrir	because, before, for, present
fyrr	before, for
fýsir	desire
fýsist	desire

G, g

Old Norse	English
gæfa	gave
gæfumaðr	gifted-man
gaf	gave, have
gaft	gave
ganga	going, to-go
gangi	come
gef	give
gefa	give
gefir	gave, give
gefit	gave, given
gefr	gives
gekk	going, went
gengi	went
gengr	went
gengu	went
gera	did, do, made, make
gerast	be
gerðist	did
gerir	did, made
gersimar	treasure
gersimi	treasure, treasured
gert	done
getit	told-of
giftu	give
giftumaðr	gifted-man
gjafar	gifts
gjöfina	the-gift
gjöfinni	the-gift
góða	good
góðar	good
góðs	good
göfgum	noble
gott	good
Grænlandi	Greenland (place)
Grænlands	Greenland (place)
grunar	suspect
Guð	God (name)
gull	gold
Gyðuson	Gyduson (name)

H, h

Old Norse	English
hætt	at-risk
haf	sea
hafa	have
hafði	had
hafir	have
hafna	harbour
haldit	holding
hálft	half
handar	hand
hann	he, he himself, him
hans	him, his
Haraldi	Harald (name)
Haraldr	Harald (name)
Haralds	Harald (name)
heðan	from-here, hence
hefi	have
hefir	had, has, have
hefta	stop
heill	whole
heit	promise
helda	held
heldr	hold, rather
hendi	hand
hér	here
herbergi	a-room
herra	lord
hét	named, promised
heyrt	heard
hingat	there
hirðin	courtiers, the-courtiers
hirðina	guardsmen
hirðmenninir	the-courtiers
hitt	find
hitta	meet
hlæja	laugh
hlógu	laughed
hluta	lot, lots
hlutrinn	thing
höfum	have
höllina	the-hall

Word List (Old Norse to English)

Old Norse	English
hönd	hand
honum	he, him, to-him
hríð	awhile
hring	a-ring, ring
hringinn	the-ring
hringinum	the-ring
hvárt	how, whether
hvárttveggja	either-way
hvat	what
hvé	how
hverju	how
hverr	every, who
hversu	how-so
hví	why
hygg	think

I, i

Old Norse	English
illa	ill
illt	ill
inn	inside, the

Í, í

Old Norse	English
í	a, for, in, is, it, of, on, to
íhugaði	considered
Ísland	Iceland (place)
Íslandi	Iceland (place)
Íslands	Iceland (place)
íslandsferðar	Iceland-journey
Íslenzkr	Icelander (name)

J, j

Old Norse	English
játum	profess
jók	increased

K, k

Old Norse	English
kæmi	came
kæmist	comes
kann	can
kastat	cast
kaupir	bought
kemr	came
kemst	came
kenndi	knew, recognised
keyptak	purchased
keyptir	bought
kirkju	church
kirkjuskoti	church-wing
klæði	clothes
klaklaust	unhurt
knörr	a-ship
kollóttr	bald
kom	came, come
koma	came, come
komast	come
kominn	come, coming, descended
komit	come
komizt	coming
konung	the-king
konungi	the-king, the-king's
konunginn	the-king
konungr	the-king
konungs	the-king
kosit	choice
kost	benefit
kunnustu	knew-how
kvað	said
kveðit	said
kveðju	greeting
kveðr	greeted
kveðst	said
kveldit	evening
kveldsöngs	evensong
kyni	kin

L, l

Old Norse	English
lætr	had, laid
lagða	enriched
lagði	laid
land	land
landa	land, lands
landi	land

Word List (Old Norse to English)

Old Norse	English
landinu	this-land
landit	land
láta	let
laug	bath
laun	reward
launa	repay, reward, rewarded
launaði	rewarded
launar	repays
launat	repaid, rewarded
lauss	less
leðrhosu	leather-purse
leggja	grant, granted
leið	journey, passed
leiðar	the-way
leiðir	led, took
leigir	rented
lét	had
letja	discourage
lézt	let, said
liðu	passed
líf	life
liggja	lay-out
líta	look
lítr	looked
lítt	little
lízt	appears
lóga	lose
lokit	ended

M, m

Old Norse	English
má	may
maðr	a-man, man
maðrinn	a-man
mælt	said, spoken
mælti	spoke
Mæri	Moer (place)
mætta	might
magran	thin
makligt	proper
mann	a-man, man
manni	man, people
mannliga	man-like
margir	many
mataðist	ate
matar	food
máttu	might
með	along, with
meðan	while
mega	may
meira	more
menn	people
mér	me, to-me
mestan	most
mesti	most
meta	value
mik	I, me, to-me
mikil	much
mikinn	a-great, much
mikit	great, much
mikla	much
miklar	much
miklu	much
milli	between
mín	me, mine
minni	mine
mislíka	mislike
mitt	mine
mjök	much
móðir	mother
móður	mother
mönnum	people
mörgum	many
móti	meeting, return
mun	could, shall, should
mundu	would
muni	shall
munir	should
muntu	shall-you
mynda	should, would
myndi	should, would

N, n

Old Norse	English
náðu	reached
nauðsyn	necessary
nema	except
niðr	down
nökkurar	some

Word List (Old Norse to English)

Old Norse	English
nökkurra	some
nökkurum	some
nökkut	sometime
Nóreg	Norway (place)
Nóregi	Norway (place)
Nóregs	Norway (place)
nú	not, now
nýtr	benefit

O, o

of	of, over, to
ofan	over-to
ok	also, and
orðit	become
oss	us

Ó, ó

ófrið	un-peace
ór	out-of
ósælligr	unhappy
óvinr	un-friend
óvitr	unwise

Ö, ö

öðru	other
öllu	all
öræfi	wild

P, p

páskum	Easter
penningr	penny

R, r

ráð	course
ráða	advise
ráði	decided
reiðfara	voyage
réttara	righter
Rómaborg	Rome-city (place)
rúmferla	Rome-travellers
rúmferlum	Rome-travellers

S, s

Old Norse	English
sá	saw, so
sættast	reconciled
sagði	said, said
sagt	said, told
sál	soul
saman	the-same
sannligt	true-like
satt	TRUE
sáumst	saw
Saxland	Saxon-lands (place)
sé	is
seg	say
segir	said, says, told
seint	coldly
seldi	handed-over
selja	sell
selr	sell
sem	as, since, such, that, what
sendir	sent
sér	he, him, himself, his, themselves, to-you, yourself
sét	seen
settak	intended
sezt	sit
síðan	after, afterwards, since, then
siðr	custom
sik	himself
silfr	silver
silfri	silver
sín	him
sína	his
sinn	his
sinnar	his
sinni	he, his, on-the-way

Word List (Old Norse to English)

Old Norse	English
sitt	his
sjá	seen, so
skal	shall
skaltu	shall
skapi	mind
skilðist	separated
skip	ship, ships, the-ship
skipaði	directed
skipazt	changed
skipi	ship, the-ship
skipinu	the-ship
skipit	ship, the-ship
skipsbrotum	ship-wreck
skipum	ships
skreppu	pouch
skulu	shall
skutilsvein	cup-bearer
skutilsveinn	cup-bearer
slík	such
slíka	such
slíku	such
sóma	honour
sómir	honourable
sótt	sickness
spurði	asked
spurt	heard
staddr	standing
staf	staff
stafkarls	the-beggar's
stafkarlsstíg	beggar's-path
starfaði	worked
stíg	path
stigi	climbed
stóðu	stood
stórmannligt	great-man-like
stund	awhile
stundir	time
stýrimanni	skipper
stýrimanns	skipper
suðr	south
suðrgöngu	south-going
sumarit	summer
svá	so, such
svarar	answered
Svein	Svein (name)
Sveini	Svein (name)
Sveinn	Svein (name)
Sveins	Svein (name), Svein's (name)
Svíþjóðar	Sweden (place)
sýnist	considered, seems

T, t

Old Norse	English
taka	take
tálma	prevent
tekr	taking, took
tíðir	a-time
tígnum	dignified, noble
til	for, to, until
tók	received, took
troði	treads
tvau	twice
týnda	lose
týnir	lose

Þ, þ

Old Norse	English
þá	then
þakkaði	thanked
þakki	thank
þangat	from-here, there
þann	then, this
þar	then, there
þars	there
þat	it, that
þegar	as-soon-as, from-there, straight-away
þegit	received
þeim	them, then, they
þeir	there, they
þeiri	there
þekkði	noticed
þekkist	knew
þenna	this
þér	to-you, you, your
þess	this
þessa	this
þessi	this

Word List (Old Norse to English)

Old Norse	English
þessu	this
þessum	this
þetta	this
þiggja	accept
þik	you
þína	you, yours
þinnar	your
þit	you
þó	though
þökk	thanks
þorði	dared
Þóri	Thorir (name)
Þóris	Thorir (name)
Þorsteini	Thorstein (name)
Þorsteinn	Thorstein (name)
Þorsteins	Thorstein (name)
þótt	though
þótti	thought
þóttist	thought
þriggja	three
þú	you
þurfti	needed
þurfuð	need
því	accordingly, because, for, then, therefore
þykkist	think
þykkja	think
þykkjast	seem

U, u

Old Norse	English
um	about, around
umbráði	managed
umsjá	about-see
undarliga	strange
unz	until
upp	up
uppi	up

Ú, ú

Old Norse	English
út	out
útan	out
útanferðina	out-travelling
úti	outside

V, v

Old Norse	English
væri	should-be
værir	would-be
valdi	will
var	as, was
varði	was
varit	wares
várit	spring
varla	hardly
varnað	wares
várr	our
váru	were
veik	turned-to
veit	knew
vel	well
ver	be
vér	we
vera	be, was
verð	worth
verða	be, become, was
verði	be, worth
verðr	was
Vestfirzkr	Westfjords (place)
vestr	west
vetra	winters
vetrinn	winter
við	at, with
víða	widely
Vík	Vik (place)
vil	will, wish
vilda	wish
vildi	wished
vildir	wish
vilið	wish
vill	wish, wished, wishes
villtu	will, will-you
virðing	worth
vist	hospitality
víst	certainly
vista	provisions
vistir	provisions
vit	we

Word List (Old Norse to English)

Old Norse	English
vita	know

Y, y

| *yðr* | you, your |
| *yðru* | your, yours |

Ý, ý

| *ýmissa* | various |

Word List *(English to Old Norse)*

English	Old Norse	English	Old Norse
		a-time	*tíðir*
		around	*um*
		about-see	*umsjá*

A, a

English	Old Norse
a	*á, á*
about	*á, á, á*
an	*á*
and	*á, á, á*
after	*áðr, áðr, ætla*
Aki (name)	*Áka, ákafliga*
all-prepared	*albúit*
all-longer	*álengðar*
all	*alla, allan, allri, allt, at*
at	*at, at*
Audun (name)	*Auðun, Auðunar, Auðuni, Auðunn*
asked	*bað, bað, báðir, bæði*
a-bear	*bjarndýri*
aid	*björg*
away	*braut, brott*
a-farm	*bú*
a-beast	*dýrit*
animal	*dýrit*
afterwards	*eftir, eftir*
am	*em*
as	*er, er, er*
are	*ert*
are-you	*ertu*
at-risk	*hætt*
a-room	*herbergi*
awhile	*hríð, hring*
a-ring	*hring*
a-ship	*knörr*
appears	*lízt*
a-man	*maðr, maðr, maðrinn*
ate	*mataðist*
along	*með*
a-great	*mikinn*
also	*ok*
advise	*ráða*
answered	*svarar*
as-soon-as	*þegar*
accept	*þiggja*
accordingly	*því*

B, b

English	Old Norse
be	*á, á, á, á, áðr, áðr*
before	*áðr, ætla, ætlaðak, ætlaði*
back	*aftr*
by	*at*
bid	*bað, báðir, bæði*
both	*báðir, bæði*
bear	*berast, betr, bezt*
better	*betr*
best	*bezt*
begging	*biðja*
break	*bryti*
beast	*dýrit*
behind	*eftir*
but	*en*
bring	*færa, færi*
beautifully	*fagrliga*
beautiful	*fögru*
because	*fyrir, fyrir*
bought	*kaupir, kemr*
bald	*kollóttr*
benefit	*kost, kunnustu*
bath	*laug*
between	*milli*
become	*orðit, páskum*
beggar's-path	*stafkarlsstíg*

C, c

English	Old Norse
carry-out	*efna*
cargo	*farmi, fé*
carried	*flytja*
confidence	*frama*
come	*gangi, gef, gefa, gefir, gefir, gefit*

Word List (English to Old Norse)

English	*Old Norse*
courtiers	*hirðin*
considered	*íhugaði, illa*
came	*kæmi, kæmist, kann, kastat, kaupir*
comes	*kæmist*
can	*kann*
cast	*kastat*
church	*kirkju*
church-wing	*kirkjuskoti*
clothes	*klæði*
coming	*kominn, kominn*
choice	*kosit*
could	*mun*
course	*ráð*
coldly	*seint*
custom	*siðr*
changed	*skipazt*
cup-bearer	*skutilsvein, skutilsveinn*
climbed	*stigi*
certainly	*víst*

D, d

day	*dag*
Denmark (place)	*Danmerkr, Danmörk*
die	*deyja*
drink	*drekk*
drew	*dró*
drinking	*drykkju*
dwelled	*dvalizt*
desire	*fýsir, fýsist*
did	*gera, gera, gera*
do	*gera*
done	*gert*
descended	*kominn*
discourage	*letja*
down	*niðr*
decided	*ráði*
directed	*skipaði*
dared	*þorði*
dignified	*tígnum*

E, e

evening	*aftaninn, aftr*
extremely	*ákafliga*
eyesight	*augsýn*
east	*austr*
Eastern-lands (place)	*Austrveg*
either-way	*hvárttveggja*
every	*hverr*
evensong	*kveldsöngs*
enriched	*lagða*
ended	*lokit*
except	*nema*
Easter	*páskum*

F, f

for	*á, á, á, áðr, áðr, ætla, ætlaðak*
from	*af, aftaninn, aftr*
farmer	*búanda*
found	*fannt, farit, farit*
fared	*farit*
fee-little	*félítill*
fell	*fell*
fields	*fjörðum*
feet	*fóta*
forth	*fram*
full	*fulla*
from-here	*heðan, heðan*
find	*hitt*
food	*matar*
from-there	*þegar*

G, g

greatly	*ágætliga*
get	*fá*
give	*fá, fær, færa, færi, fagrliga*
go	*fær*
gone	*farit*
gave	*gæfa, gæfumaðr, gaf, gaf, gaft*

Word List (English to Old Norse)

English	Old Norse	English	Old Norse
gifted-man	gæfumaðr, gaf	hold	heldr
going	ganga, gangi	here	hér
given	gefit	heard	heyrt, hirðin
gives	gefr	how	hvárt, hvárttveggja, hvé
gifts	gjafar	how-so	hversu
good	góða, góðar, góðs, gott	handed-over	seldi
Greenland (place)	Grænlandi, Grænlands	himself	sér, sér
God (name)	Guð	honour	sóma
gold	gull	honourable	sómir
Gyduson (name)	Gyðuson	hardly	varla
guardsmen	hirðina	hospitality	vist
greeting	kveðju		
greeted	kveðr		
grant	leggja		
granted	leggja		
great	mikit		
great-man-like	stórmannligt		

H, h

English	Old Norse
had	ætta, ætta, af, aftaninn, aftr, ágætliga
have	ætta, af, aftaninn, aftr, ágætliga, Áka, ákafliga, Áki
have-you	áttu
help	björg
harbour	hafna
holding	haldit
half	hálft
hand	handar, hann, hann
he	hann, hann, hann, hans
he himself	hann
him	hann, hans, hans, Haraldi, Haraldr
his	hans, Haraldi, Haraldr, Haralds, heðan, heðan, hefi
Harald (name)	Haraldi, Haraldr, Haralds
hence	heðan
has	hefir
held	helda

I, i

English	Old Norse
in	á, á
it	á, áðr, áðr, ætla, ætlaðak
intend	ætla, ætlaðak
intended	ætlaðak, ætlaði, ætlar, ætlar, ætlat
in-drink	drukknir
if	ef
I	ek, em, en
is	er, ert, ertu
ill	illa, illt
inside	inn
Iceland (place)	Ísland, Íslandi, Íslands
Iceland-journey	Íslandsferðar
Icelander (name)	Íslenzkr
increased	jók

J, j

English	Old Norse
joyfulness	blíðu
journey	ferðar, finna

K, k

English	Old Norse
killed	drepinn
knew	kenndi, keyptir, kirkju
knew-how	kunnustu
kin	kyni
know	vita

Word List (English to Old Norse)

English	*Old Norse*

L, l

lord	*herra*
laugh	*hlæja*
laughed	*hlógu*
lot	*hluta*
lots	*hluta*
laid	*lætr, lagða*
land	*land, landa, landa, landi*
lands	*landa*
let	*láta, laug*
less	*lauss*
leather-purse	*leðrhosu*
led	*leiðir*
life	*líf*
lay-out	*liggja*
look	*líta*
looked	*lítr*
little	*lítt*
lose	*lóga, lokit, má*

M, m

money	*fé, félausan*
money-less	*félausan, félauss*
more	*fleira, flytja*
meet	*fund, fundar, fundit*
met	*fundit*
made	*gera, gera*
make	*gera*
may	*má, maðr*
man	*maðr, maðrinn, Mæri*
Moer (place)	*Mæri*
might	*mætta, mann*
man-like	*mannliga*
many	*margir, mataðist*
me	*mér, mestan, mesti*
most	*mestan, mesti*
much	*mikil, mikinn, mikinn, mikit, mikit, mikla, miklar*
mine	*mín, minni, mislíka*
mislike	*mislíka*
mother	*móðir, móður*
meeting	*móti*
mind	*skapi*
managed	*umbráði*

N, n

never	*aldrigi*
not	*eiga, eiga, eiga, eigi*
none	*eigi, eigi*
noble	*göfgum, grunar*
named	*hét*
necessary	*nauðsyn*
Norway (place)	*Nóreg, Nóregi, Nóregs*
now	*nú*
noticed	*þekkði*
needed	*þurfti*
need	*þurfuð*

O, o

of	*á, á, á, á*
on	*á, á*
others	*aðrir, af*
off	*af*
out-of	*af, aftr*
or	*eða*
own	*eiga, eiga*
owned	*eiga, eigi, eigi*
one-such	*einhverju*
one	*einn, einu, eitt, eitthvert*
of-wealth	*fjárins*
other	*öðru*
over	*of*
over-to	*ofan*
on-the-way	*sinni*
out	*út, útan*
out-travelling	*útanferðina*
outside	*úti*
our	*várr*

Word List (English to Old Norse)

English	*Old Norse*	English	*Old Norse*

P, p

prepared	*búa, búast, búit*
peace	*friði*
present	*fyrir*
promise	*heit*
promised	*hét*
profess	*játum*
purchased	*keyptak*
passed	*leið, leiðar*
proper	*makligt*
people	*manni, með, meðan*
penny	*penningr*
pouch	*skreppu*
path	*stíg*
prevent	*tálma*
provisions	*vista, vistir*

Q, q

quay	*bryggjur*

R, r

returning	*aftr*
rather	*heldr*
ring	*hring*
recognised	*kenndi*
reward	*laun, launa*
repay	*launa*
rewarded	*launa, launaði, launar*
repays	*launar*
repaid	*launat*
rented	*leigir*
return	*móti*
reached	*náðu*
righter	*réttara*
Rome-city (place)	*Rómaborg*
Rome-travellers	*rúmferla, rúmferlum*
reconciled	*sættast*
received	*þegit, þeim*

S, s

steward	*ármaðrinn, ármanni*
soon	*brátt*
settled	*búit*
some-kind	*eitthvert*
suspect	*grunar*
sea	*haf*
stop	*hefta*
said	*kvað, kveðit, kveðst, landinu, laun, launa, launa, launa, launaði*
spoken	*mælt*
spoke	*mælti*
shall	*mun, mun, mundu, muni, munir*
should	*mun, mundu, muni, munir*
shall-you	*muntu*
some	*nökkurar, nökkurra, nökkurum*
sometime	*nökkut*
saw	*sá, sá*
so	*sá, sættast, sagði*
soul	*sál*
Saxon-lands (place)	*Saxland*
say	*seg*
says	*segir*
sell	*selja, selr*
since	*sem, sem*
such	*sem, sem, sem, sendir, sér*
sent	*sendir*
seen	*sét, sezt*
sit	*sezt*
silver	*silfr, silfri*
separated	*skilðist*
ship	*skip, skip, skip*
ships	*skip, skip*
ship-wreck	*skipsbrotum*
sickness	*sótt*
standing	*staddr*
staff	*staf*
stood	*stóðu*
skipper	*stýrimanni, stýrimanns*
south	*suðr*

Word List (English to Old Norse)

English	*Old Norse*	English	*Old Norse*
south-going	*suðrgöngu*	the-king	*konung, konungi, konungi, konunginn, konungr*
summer	*sumarit*		
Svein (name)	*Svein, Sveini, Sveinn, Sveins*	the-king's	*konungi*
Svein's (name)	*Sveins*	this-land	*landinu*
Sweden (place)	*Svíþjóðar*	the-way	*leiðar*
seems	*sýnist*	took	*leiðir, leigir, lézt*
straight-away	*þegar*	thin	*magran*
seem	*þykkjast*	to-me	*mér, meta*
strange	*undarliga*	told	*sagt, sál*
should-be	*væri*	the-same	*saman*
spring	*várit*	true-like	*sannligt*
		true	
		themselves	*sér*
		to-you	*sér, sér*
		the-ship	*skip, skipi, skipi, skipinu*

T, t

English	*Old Norse*	English	*Old Norse*
that	*á, á, á, aðrir, af, af*	the-beggar's	*stafkarls*
the	*á, á, aðrir*	time	*stundir*
to	*á, aðrir, af, af, af*	take	*taka*
the-steward	*ármanni*	taking	*tekr*
the-bear	*bjarndýrit*	thanked	*þakkaði*
table	*borðinu*	thank	*þakki*
the-beast	*dýrit, dýrsins*	this	*þann, þar, þar, þars, þat, þegar, þegit, þeim*
than	*en*		
then	*en, engu, enn, enn, er, er, er, er*	them	*þeim*
		they	*þeim, þeir*
they-are	*eru*	though	*þó, þökk*
travelled	*færa, færir, far, fara, fara*	thanks	*þökk*
		Thorir (name)	*Þóri, Þóris*
travel	*færir, far, fara, fara, farir, féit*	Thorstein (name)	*Þorsteini, Þorsteinn, Þorsteins*
treasure	*féit, fénu, ferð*	thought	*þótti, þóttist*
travelling	*ferðarinnar*	three	*þriggja*
to-meet	*finna*	therefore	*því*
to-go	*ganga*	treads	*troði*
treasured	*gersimi*	twice	*tvau*
told-of	*getit*	turned-to	*veik*
the-gift	*gjöfina, gjöfinni*		
there	*hingat, hirðin, hirðmenninir, hlutrinn, höllina, honum*		

U, u

English	*Old Norse*
unhurt	*klaklaust*
un-peace	*ófrið*
unhappy	*ósælligr*
us	*oss*

English	*Old Norse*
the-courtiers	*hirðin, hirðmenninir*
thing	*hlutrinn*
the-hall	*höllina*
to-him	*honum*
the-ring	*hringinn, hringinum*
think	*hygg, í, í*

Word List (English to Old Norse)

English	*Old Norse*	English	*Old Norse*
un-friend	*óvinr*	wish	*vil, vilda, vildi, vildir, vilið*
unwise	*óvitr*		
until	*til, tók*	wished	*vildi, vildir*
up	*upp, uppi*	wishes	*vill*
		will-you	*villtu*

V, v

value	*meta*
voyage	*reiðfara*
Vik (place)	*Vík*
various	*ýmissa*

Y, y

yourself	*sér*
you	*þér, þér, þess, þessa, þessi, þessu*
your	*þér, þess, þessa, þessi*
yours	*þína, þinnar*

W, w

wrecked	*brjótir, bryggjur*
wild-animal	*dýr*
was	*er, er, er, er, er, eru*
what	*er, er, er*
when	*er*
which	*er*
who	*er, eru*
were	*eru, færa*
wealth	*fénu, ferð*
went	*gekk, gengi, gengr, gengu*
whole	*heill*
whether	*hvárt*
why	*hví*
with	*með, meðan*
while	*meðan*
would	*mundu, muni, munir*
wild	*öræfi*
worked	*starfaði*
would-be	*værir*
will	*valdi, var, varði*
wares	*varit, várit*
well	*vel*
we	*vér, vera*
worth	*verð, verða, verði*
Westfjords (place)	*Vestfirzkr*
west	*vestr*
winters	*vetra*
winter	*vetrinn*
widely	*víða*

The Tale of Auðun of the West Fjords (*Old Icelandic*)

Auðunar þáttur vestfirska, from the Flateyjarbók (GkS 1005 fol., c. 1390, Árni Magnússon Institute for Icelandic Studies)

Old Icelandic	Literal	English
1	**1**	**1**
Maður hét Auðun, vestfirskur að kyni og félítill.	Man named Audun, Westfjords by kin and fee-little.	There was a man named Audun, from the West Fjords by kin, and he was poor.
Hann fór utan vestur þar í fjörðum með umráði Þorsteins búanda góðs og Þóris stýrimanns er þar hafði þegið vist of veturinn með Þorsteini.	He travelled out west there in fields with managed Thorstein farmer good and Thorir skipper who there had received hospitality over winter with Thorstein.	He travelled west to the fields which were managed by Thorstein, a good farmer, and Thorir who was a skipper, and they received hospitality from Thorstein over the winter.
Auðun var og þar og starfaði fyrir honum Þóri og þá þessi laun af honum, utanferðina og hans umsjá.	Audun was also there and worked for him Thorir and then this reward of him, out-travelling and him about-see.	Audun was also there and worked for Thorir, and was rewarded by him with a place on his voyage, and taking care of him.
Hann Auðun lagði mestan hluta fjár þess er var fyrir móður sína áður hann stigi á skip og var kveðið á þriggja vetra björg.	He Audun laid most lot wealth this that was for mother his after he climbed on the-ship and was said of three winters aid.	Audun gave most of his wealth that was for his mother, once he had gone aboard the ship, and it was said to be three winters' worth of aid.
Og nú fara þeir út héðan og ferst þeim vel og var Auðun of veturinn eftir með Þóri stýrimanni.	And now travelled they out hence and travelled they well and was Audun of winter afterwards with Thorir skipper.	And now they travelled out from there, and they travelled well, and Audun spent the winter afterwards with the skipper Thorir.
Hann átti bú á Mæri.	He had a-farm in Moer.	He had a farm in Moer.
Og um sumarið eftir fara þeir út til Grænlands og eru þar of veturinn.	And about summer afterwards travelled they out to Greenland and were there of winter.	And around the summer afterwards they travelled out to Greenland and were there for the winter.

The Tale of Auðun of the West Fjords (Old Icelandic)

Old Icelandic	Literal	English
Þess er við getið að Auðun kaupir þar bjarndýri eitt, gersemi mikla, og gaf þar fyrir alla eigu sína.	This is with told-of that Audun bought there a-bear one, treasured much, and have there for all owned his.	It is told that Audun bought a bear there, which was much treasured, and gave all that he owned for it.
Og nú of sumarið eftir þá fara þeir aftur til Noregs og verða vel reiðfara.	And now of summer afterwards then travelled they returning to Norway and was well voyage.	And now about the summer afterwards then they travelled returning to Norway and the voyage went well.
Hefir Auðun dýr sitt með sér og ætlar nú að fara suður til Danmerkur á fund Sveins konungs og gefa honum dýrið.	Had Audun wild-animal his with him and intended now to travel south to Denmark to meet Svein the-king and give him the-beast.	Audun had his wild-animal with him and intended now to travel south to Denmark to meet King Svein and give him the beast.
Og er hann kom suður í landið þar sem konungur var fyrir þá gengur hann upp af skipi og leiðir eftir sér dýrið og leigir sér herbergi.	And as he came south to land there as the-king was present then went he up off the-ship and took behind him the-beast and rented himself a-room.	And as he came south to land, where the king was present, he then went up off the ship and took the beast with him and rented himself a room.
Haraldi konungi var sagt brátt að þar var komið bjarndýri, gersemi mikil, og á íslenskur maður.	Harald the-king was told soon that there was come a-bear, treasured much, and an Icelander man.	King Harald was soon told, that a bear had come, which was much treasured, and an Icelander.
Konungur sendir þegar menn eftir honum.	The-king sent straight-away people after him.	The king sent people to fetch him straight away,
Og er Auðun kom fyrir konung kveður hann konung vel.	And as Audun came before the-king greeted he the-king well.	and when Audun came before the king, he greeted the king well.
Konungur tók vel kveðju hans og spurði síðan:	The-king took well greeting his and asked afterwards:	The king received his greeting well and afterwards asked:
"Áttu gersemi mikla í bjarndýri?"	"Have-you treasured much a bear?"	"Do you have a bear which is much treasured?".
Hann svarar og kveðst eiga dýrið eitthvert.	He answered and said owned a-beast some-kind.	He answered and said that he owned a beast of some kind.
Konungur mælti:	The-king spoke:	The king spoke:
"Viltu selja oss dýrið við slíku verði sem þú keyptir?"	"Will-you sell us the-beast with such worth as you bought?"	"Will you sell us the beast for the same worth as you bought it?".
Hann svarar:	He answered:	He answered:

The Tale of Auðun of the West Fjords (Old Icelandic)

Old Icelandic	Literal	English
"Eigi vil eg það herra".	"Not wish i that lord".	"I do not wish to do that, lord".
"Viltu þá", segir konungur, "að eg gefi þér tvö verð slík og mun það réttara ef þú hefir þar við gefið alla þína eigu?"	"Will-you then" said the-king, "that i give to-you twice worth such and should that righter if you have there with given all you own?"	"Do you wish then", said the king, "that I give you twice the worth, and that should be right, if you have given all you own for it?".
"Eigi vil eg það herra", segir hann.	"Not wish i that lord" said he.	"I do not wish to do that, lord", he said.
Konungur mælti:	The-king spoke:	The king spoke:
"Viltu gefa mér þá?"	"Will-you give me then?"	"Will you give it to me then?".
Hann svarar:	He answered:	He answered:
"Eigi herra".	"Not lord".	"I will not, lord".
Konungur mælti:	The-king spoke:	The king spoke:
"Hvað viltu þá af gera?"	"What will-you then of do?"	"What do you wish to do then?".
Hann svarar:	He answered:	He answered:
"Fara suður til Danmerkur og gefa Sveini konungi".	"Travel south to Denmark and give Svein the-king".	"Travel", said he, to Denmark and give it to King Svein".
Haraldur konungur segir:	Harald the-king said:	King Harald said:
"Hvort er að þú ert maður svo óvitur að þú hefir eigi heyrt ófrið þann er í milli er landa þessa eða ætlar þú giftu þína svo mikla að þú munir þar komast með gersemar er aðrir fá eigi komist klakklaust þó að nauðsyn eigi til?"	"Whether is that you are a-man so unwise that you have none heard un-peace then that is between the land this or intend you give yours so much that you should there come with treasure that others get none coming unhurt though that necessary not to?"	"Is it possible, that you are an unwise man, that you have not heard of the state of war that is between these lands, or you suppose that you are so gifted that you would come there with treasure, where others have not gone unhurt though it was necessary?".
Auðun svarar:	Audun answered:	Audun answered:
"Herra það er á yðru valdi en öngu játum vér öðru en þessu er vér höfum áður ætlað".	"Lord that is for your will but none profess we other than this that we have before intended".	"That is for your will lord, but I cannot agree to anything other than what I have previously intended".

The Tale of Auðun of the West Fjords (Old Icelandic)

Old Icelandic	Literal	English
Þá mælti konungur:	Then spoke the-king:	Then the king spoke:
"Hví mun eigi það til að þú farir leið þína sem þú vilt og kom þá til mín er þú ferð aftur og seg mér hversu Sveinn konungur launar þér dýrið. Og kann það vera að þú sért gæfumaður".	"Why should not that to that you travel journey yours as you wish and come then to me that you travel back and say to-me how-so Svein the-king repays your beast. And can that be that you yourself gifted-man".	"Then why should you not, to travel on your journey, as you wish, and then come to me, when you travel back, and tell me how King Svein repays you for the beast, and can it be, that you will be a gifted man".
"Því heiti eg þér", sagði Auðun.	"Accordingly promise i to-you" said Audun.	"I promise this to you accordingly", said Audun.
Hann fer nú síðan suður með landi og í Vík austur og þá til Danmerkur og er þá uppi hver peningur fjárins og verður hann þá biðja matar bæði fyrir sig og fyrir dýrið.	He travelled now afterwards south along land and to Vik east and then to Denmark and was then up every penny of-wealth and was he then begging food both for himself and for the-beast.	He now travelled afterwards south along the land and to Vik east and then to Denmark, and then every penny of his wealth was spent, and he was then begging for food both for himself and for the beast.
Hann kemur á fund ármanns Sveins konungs þess er Áki hét og bað hann vista nakkvarra bæði fyrir sig og fyrir dýrið.	He came to meet steward Svein's the-king this was Aki named and asked him provisions some asked for himself and for the-beast.	He came to meet a steward of King Svein, who was named Aki, and he asked him for some provisions for himself and for the beast,
"Eg ætla", segir hann, "að gefa Sveini konungi dýrið".	"I intend" said he, "to give Svein the-king the-beast".	I intend, he said, "to give this beast to King Svein".
Áki lést selja mundu honum vistir ef hann vildi.	Aki said sell would him provisions if he wished.	Aki said that he would sell him provisions if he wished.
Auðun kveðst ekki til hafa fyrir að gefa "en eg vildi þó", segir hann, "að þetta kæmist til leiðar að eg mætti dýrið færa konungi".	Audun said not to have for to give "and i wish though" said he, "that this comes to the-way that i might the-beast bring the-king".	Audun said that he did not have anything to give, "and though I wish", he said, "that I may be able t bring this beast to the king".
"Eg mun fá þér vistir sem þið þurfið til konungs fundar en þar í móti vil eg eiga hálft dýrið og máttu á það líta að dýrið mun deyja fyrir þér þars þið þurfið vistir miklar en fé sé farið og er búið við að þú hafir þá ekki dýrsins".	"I shall give you provisions that you need to the-king meet then there on meeting will i own half the-beast and might be that look that the-beast could die for you there you need provisions much but money is gone and is settled with that you have then not the-beast".	"I shall give you provisions, that you need to meet the king, then on meeting him I will own half the beast, otherwise it might be, that the beast could die before you, there you will need many provisions, but your money is gone, and it shall be that you will then not have the beast".

The Tale of Auðun of the West Fjords (Old Icelandic)

Old Icelandic	Literal	English
Og er hann lítur á þetta sýnist honum nokkuð eftir sem ármaðurinn mælti fyrir honum og sættast þeir á þetta að hann selur Áka hálft dýrið og skal konungur síðan meta allt saman.	And when he looked a this considered he sometime afterwards what steward spoke before him and reconciled they to this that he sell Aki half the-beast and shall the-king afterwards value all the-same.	And when he looked at this, he considered for some time afterwards what the steward had said to him, and they reconciled to this, that he would sell Aki half of the beast, and the king would afterwards value it all the same.
Skulu þeir fara báðir nú á fund konungs. Og svo gera þeir, fara nú báðir á fund konungs og stóðu fyrir borðinu.	Shall they travel both now and meet the-king. And so did they, travelled now both to meet the-king and stood before table.	And should they now both travel and meet the king, and they did so, they both travelled to meet the king and stood before his tables.
Konungur íhugaði hver þessi maður mundi vera er hann kenndi eigi og mælti síðan til Auðunar:	The-king considered who this man should be that he knew not and spoke then to Audun:	The king considered, who this man should be, that he did not know, and then spoke to Audun:
"Hver ertu?" segir hann.	"Who are-you?" said he.	"Who are you?" he said.
Hann svarar:	He answered:	He answered:
"Eg em íslenskur maður herra", segir hann, "og kominn nú utan af Grænlandi og nú af Noregi og ætlaði eg að færa yður bjarndýr þetta.	"I am Icelander man lord" said he, "and coming now out out-of Greenland and now from Norway and intended I to bring your bear this.	"I am an Icelander, lord", he said, "and I have come from Greenland and from Norway intending to bring you this bear.
Keypti eg það með allri eigu minni og nú er þó á orðið mikið fyrir mér, eg á nú hálft eitt dýrið" og segir síðan konungi hversu farið hafði með þeim Áka ármanni hans.	Purchased I it with all own mine and now is though that become much for me, i of not half one beast" and told after the-king how-so fared had with them Aki the-steward his.	I purchased it with all that I own, and now though it has become much for me, I do not own half of the beast", and he then told the king, how it had gone with Aki, his steward.
Konungur mælti:	The-king spoke:	The king spoke:
"Er það satt Áki er hann segir?"	"Is that true Aki what he says?"	"Is that true, Aki, what he says?".
"Satt er það", segir hann.	"True is that" said he.	"That is true", he said.
Konungur mælti:	The-king spoke:	The king spoke:

The Tale of Auðun of the West Fjords (Old Icelandic)

Old Icelandic	Literal	English
"Og þótti þér það til liggja þar sem eg setti þig mikinn mann að hefta það eða tálma er maður gerðist til að færa mér gersemi og gaf fyrir alla eign og sá það Haraldur konungur að ráði að láta hann fara í friði og er hann vor óvinur?	"And thought you that to lay-out then since i intended you a-great man to stop that or prevent as a-man did to that bring to-me treasure and gave because all owned and so that Harald the-king that decided to let him travel in peace and that he our un-friend?	"And you thought to let this happen, even though I intended you to be a great man, to stop or prevent, as a man made to bring this treasure and give to me all that he owned, and even though King Harald decided to let him travel in peace, even though he is our enemy?
Hygg þú að þá hve sannlegt það var þinnar handar og það væri maklegt að þú værir drepinn.	Think you that then how true-like that was your hand and that should-be proper that you would-be killed.	Think then how true your hand was, and it would be right, that you should be killed.
En eg mun nú eigi það gera en braut skaltu fara þegar úr landinu og koma aldregi aftur síðan mér í augsýn.	But i should now not that do but away shall travel straight-away out-of this-land and come never back after to-me in eyesight.	I will not do what I should, but you shall travel away immediately out of this land and never come back in my sight.
En þér Auðun kann eg slíka þökk sem þú gefir mér allt dýrið og ver hér með mér".	But you Audun can i such thanks as you gave me all animal and be here with me".	But you, Audun, can I thank such as you gave me the whole animal, and be here with me".
Það þekkist hann og er með Sveini konungi um hríð.	That knew he and was with Svein the-king about awhile.	That he knew, and he was with King Svein for a while.

2

Old Icelandic	Literal	English
Og er liðu nakkverjar stundir þá mælti Auðun við konung:	And as passed some time then spoke Audun with the-king:	And as some time has passed, then Audun spoke with the king:
"Braut fýsir mig nú herra".	"Away desire me now lord".	"I desire now to travel away, lord".
Konungur svarar heldur seint:	The-king answered rather coldly:	The king answered rather coldly:
"Hvað viltu þá", segir hann, "ef þú vilt eigi með oss vera?"	"What will-you then" said he, "if you wish not with us be?"	"What do you wish for then", he said, "if not to be with us?".
Hann svarar:	He answered:	He said:
"Suður vil eg ganga".	"South wish i to-go".	"I wish to go south".

The Tale of Auðun of the West Fjords (Old Icelandic)

Old Icelandic	Literal	English
"Ef þú vildir eigi svo gott ráð taka", segir konungur, "þá mundi mér fyrir þykja í er þú fýsist í brott".	"If you wish not so good course take" said the-king, "then would me for think it that you desire to away".	"If you did not wish to take such a good course", said the king, "I would mind it to think that you desire to go away".
Og nú gaf konungur honum silfur mjög mikið og fór hann suður síðan með Rúmferlum og skipaði konungur til um ferð hans, bað hann koma til sín er hann kæmi aftur.	And now gave the-king him silver much great and travelled he south afterwards with Rome-travellers and directed the-king to about travel his, asked him come to him when he came returning.	And now the king gave him much great silver, and he travelled south afterwards with pilgrims, and the king made arrangements for his journey, and asked him to come to him when he returned.
Nú fór hann ferðar sinnar uns hann kemur suður í Rómaborg.	Now travelled he journey his until he came south to Rome-city.	Now he travelled on his journey, until he came south to Rome.
Og er hann hefir þar dvalist sem hann tíðir þá fer hann aftur, tekur þá sótt mikla. Gerir hann þá ákaflega magran.	And as he had there dwelled such he a-time then travelled he returning, took then sickness much. Made him then extremely thin.	And when he had dwelled there for such a time, he travelled to return, and took to much sickness, which made him extremely thin.
Gengur þá upp allt féið það er konungur hafði gefið honum til ferðarinnar, tekur síðan upp stafkarls stíg og biður sér matar.	Went then up all treasure that which the-king had given him to travelling, taking afterwards up beggar's-path path and asked he food.	Gone was all his treasure, which the king had given him for travelling, and afterwards he took to begging and he asked for food.
Hann er þá kollóttur og heldur ósællegur.	He was then bald and rather unhappy.	He was then bald and rather unhappy.
Hann kemur aftur í Danmörk að páskum þangað sem konungur er þá staddur en ei þorði hann að láta sjá sig og var í kirkjuskoti og ætlaði þá til fundar við konung er hann gengi til kirkju um kveldið.	He came back to Denmark at easter there as the-king was then standing but not dared he to let seen himself and was in church-wing and intended then to meet with the-king when he went to church around evening.	He came back to Denmark at Easter, there where the king was standing, but he dared not to let himself be seen, and was in the church wing and intended to meet with the king, when he went to church in the evening.
Og nú er hann sá konunginn og hirðina fagurlega búna þá þorði hann eigi að láta sjá sig.	And now when he saw the-king and guardsmen beautifully prepared then dared he not to let seen himself.	And now when he saw the king and the guardsmen so beautifully dressed, then he dared not to let himself be seen.

The Tale of Auðun of the West Fjords (Old Icelandic)

Old Icelandic	Literal	English
Og er konungur gekk til drykkju í höllina þá mataðist Auðun úti sem siður er til Rúmferla meðan þeir hafa eigi kastað staf og skreppu.	And when the-king went to drinking in the-hall then ate Audun outside as custom is for Rome-travellers while they have not cast staff and pouch.	And when the king went drinking in the hall, Audun ate outside, which was the custom for pilgrims, while they have cast aside their staff and pouch.
Og nú of aftaninn er konungur gekk til kveldsöngs ætlaði Auðun að hitta hann. Og svo mikið sem honum þótti fyrr fyrir jók nú miklu á er þeir voru drukknir hirðmennirnir.	And now of evening as the-king going to evensong intended Audun to meet him. And so much as he thought for before increased now much for that they were in-drink the-courtiers.	And now in the evening, as the king was going to evensong, Audun intended to meet him, and as much as he had thought before was now increased, because the courtiers were drunk.
Og er þeir gengu inn aftur þá þekkti konungur mann og þóttist finna að eigi hafði frama til að ganga fram að hitta hann.	And as they went inside back then noticed the-king a-man and thought found that not had confidence to that going from to meet him.	And as they went back inside, then the king thought he noticed a man thought he found, that he did not have the confidence in going to meet him.
Og er hirðin gekk inn þá veik konungur út og mælti:	And as the-courtiers going inside then turned-to the-king out and spoke:	And now as the courtiers were going inside, then the king turned and spoke out:
"Gangi sá nú fram er mig vill finna.	"Come so now forth who me wishes to-meet.	"Come forth now, who wishes to meet me.
Mig grunar að sá muni vera maðurinn".	I suspect that so shall be a-man".	For I suspect that there is such a man".
Þá gekk Auðun fram og féll til fóta konungi og varla kenndi konungur hann.	Then went Audun forth and fell to feet the-king's and hardly recognised the-king him.	Then Audun went forth and fell at the king's feet, and the king hardly recognised him.
Og þegar er konungur veit hver hann er tók konungur í hönd honum Auðuni og bað hann velkominn "og hefir þú mikið skipast", segir hann, "síðan við sáumst", leiðir hann eftir sér inn.	And as-soon-as that the-king knew who he was took the-king in hand him Audun and asked him well "and have you much changed" said he, "since we saw" led he after him inside.	And as soon as the king knew who he was, the king took Audun in hand and bid him welcome, "and you have changed much", he said, "since we last saw each other", and after he led him inside.
Og er hirðin sá hann hlógu þeir að honum en konungur sagði:	And when courtiers saw him laughed they at him but the-king said:	And when the courtiers saw him, they laughed at him, but the king said:

The Tale of Auðun of the West Fjords (Old Icelandic)

Old Icelandic	Literal	English
"Eigi þurfið þér að honum að hlæja því að betur hefir hann séð fyrir sinni sál heldur en þér".	"None need you that him to laugh because that better has he himself seen for his soul rather than you".	"None of you need to laugh at him, because he has seen better for his soul than any of you".
Þá lét konungur gera honum laug og gaf honum síðan klæði og er hann nú með honum.	Then had the-king made him bath and gave him afterwards clothes and was he not with him.	Then the king had a bath made for him, and afterwards gave him clothes, and he was now with him.

3

Það er nú sagt einhverju sinni of vorið að konungur býður Auðuni að vera með sér álengdar og kveðst mundu gera hann skutilsvein sinn og leggja til hans góða virðing.	It is now said one-such on-the-way to spring that the-king bid Audun to be with him all-longer and said would make him cup-bearer his and grant to him good worth.	It is now said, that on the way to spring, the king invited Audun to be with him for all of his days, and said that he would make him his cup-bearer and grant him good worthiness.
Auðun segir:	Audun said:	Audun said:
"Guð þakki yður herra sóma þann allan er þér viljið til mín leggja en hitt er mér í skapi að fara út til Íslands".	"God thank you lord honour this all that you wish to me grant but find i to-me of mind to travel out to Iceland".	"God thank you, lord, for all this honour that you wish to grant me, but I find in my mind, to travel out to Iceland".
Konungur segir:	The-king said:	The king said:
"Þetta sýnist mér undarlega kosið".	"This seems to-me strange choice".	"This seems a strange choice to me".
Auðun mælti:	Audun spoke:	Audun spoke:
"Eigi má eg það vita herra", segir hann, "að eg hafi hér mikinn sóma með yður en móðir mín troði stafkarls stíg út á Íslandi því að nú er lokið björg þeirri er eg lagði til áður eg færi af Íslandi".	"Not may i that know lord" said he, "that i have here much honour with you but mother mine treads the-beggar's path out in Iceland for that now is ended help there that i enriched to before i travelled from Iceland".	"Not may I know, lord", said he, "that I have much honour here with you, but my mother treads the beggar's path out in Iceland, for now my help there is ended, that which I enriched her with, before I travelled out from Iceland".
Konungur svarar:	The-king answered:	The king answered:
"Vel er mælt", segir hann, "og mannlega og muntu verða giftumaður.	"Well is spoken" said he, "and man-like and shall-you be gifted-man.	"It is well spoken", said he, "and like a man, and you shall be a gifted man.

The Tale of Auðun of the West Fjords (Old Icelandic)

Old Icelandic	Literal	English
Sjá einn var svo hluturinn að mér mundi eigi mislíka að þú færir í braut héðan og ver nú með mér þar til er skip búast".	So one as such thing that to-me should not mislike that you travel to away from-here and be now with me then until that ship prepared".	So there is one such thing, that I should not dislike, that you travel away from here, and be now with me, then until a ship is prepared".
Hann gerir svo.	He did so.	He did so.
Einn dag er á leið vorið gekk Sveinn konungur ofan á bryggjur og voru menn þá að að búa skip til ýmissa landa, í Austurveg eða Saxland, til Svíþjóðar eða Noregs.	One day when it passed spring went Svein the-king over-to the quay and were people then about that prepared ships to various lands, in Eastern-lands or Saxon-lands, to Sweden or Norway.	One day, when spring had passed, King Svein went over to the quay, and there were people about preparing ships for various lands, Eastern-lands, Saxon-lands, to Sweden or Norway.
Þá koma þeir Auðun að einu skipi fögru og voru menn að að búa skipið.	Then came there Audun to one ship beautiful and were people that it prepared ship.	Then Audun came to a beautiful ship, and there were people that were preparing the ship.
Þá spurði konungur:	Then asked the-king:	Then the king asked:
"Hversu líst þér Auðun á þetta skip?"	"How-so appears to-you Audun about this ship?"	"How does this ship appear to you, Audun?"
Hann svarar:	He answered:	He answered:
"Vel herra".	"Well lord".	"Well lord".
Konungur mælti:	The-king spoke:	The king spoke:
"Þetta skip vil eg þér gefa og launa bjarndýrið".	"This ship wish i to-you give and reward the-bear".	"I wish to give you this ship as a reward for the bear".
Hann þakkaði gjöfina eftir sinni kunnustu.	He thanked the-gift after he knew-how.	He thanked him for the gift as well as he knew how.
Og er leið stund og skipið var albúið þá mælti Sveinn konungur við Auðun:	And when passed awhile and ship was all-prepared then spoke Svein the-king with Audun:	And when a while had passed and the ship was all prepared, then King Svein spoke with Audun:

The Tale of Auðun of the West Fjords (Old Icelandic)

Old Icelandic	Literal	English
"Þó viltu nú á braut þá mun eg nú ekki letja þig en það hefi eg spurt að illt er til hafna fyrir landi yðru og eru víða öræfi og hætt skipum.	"Though will now to away then should i now not discourage you but it have i heard that ill is to harbour for land yours and they-are widely wild and at-risk ships.	"Though you now wish to go away, then I should not now discourage you, but I have heard that bad are the harbours in your land, and they are widely wild and ships are at risk.
Nú brýtur þú og týnir skipinu og fénu.	Now wrecked you and lose the-ship and cargo.	Now should your ship be wrecked and you lose your ship and cargo.
Lítt sér það þá á að þú hafir fundið Svein konung og gefið honum gersemi".	Little to-you that then be that you have met Svein the-king and gave him treasure".	You shall have little to say that you have met King Svein and gave him treasure".
Síðan seldi konungur honum leðurhosu fulla af silfri "og ertu þá enn eigi félaus með öllu þótt þú brjótir skipið ef þú færð haldið þessu.	Afterwards handed-over the-king to-him leather-purse full of silver "and are-you then one not money-less with all though you wrecked ship if you go holding this.	Afterwards the king handed over to him a leather purse full of silver, "and are you then not penniless, even though your ship is wrecked, if you hold on to this.
Verða má svo enn" segir konungur, "að þú týnir þessu fé. Lítt nýtur þú þá þess, er þú fannst Svein konung og gafst honum gersemi".	Become may so then" said the-king, "that you lose this money. Little benefit you then this, that you found Svein the-king and gave him treasure".	But if it becomes then", said the king, "that you lose this money. It will benefit you little then, that you have met King Svein and given him treasure".
Síðan dró konungur hring af hendi sér og gaf Auðuni og mælti:	Then drew the-king a-ring of hand his and gave Audun and spoke:	Then the king drew a ring from his hand and gave it to Audun saying:
"Þó að svo illa verði að þú brjótir skipið og týnir fénu, eigi ertu félaus ef þú kemst á land því að margir menn hafa gull á sér í skipsbrotum og sér þá að þú hefir fundið Svein konung ef þú heldur hringinum.	"Though that so ill be that you wrecked ship and lose money, not are-you money-less if you came to land therefore that many people have gold about themselves for ship-wreck and yourself then that you have met Svein the-king if you hold the-ring.	"Even though it would be so bad if your ship was wrecked, and you lose all the money, you shall not be penniless, therefore many people have gold about themselves in case of being shipwrecked, and you shall have met King Svein, if you hold on to this ring.
En það vil eg ráða þér", segir hann, "að þú gefir eigi hringinn nema þú þykist eiga svo mikið gott að launa nakkverjum göfgum manni, þá gef þeim hringinn því að tignum mönnum sómir að þiggja.	But that wish i advise to-you" said he, "that you give not the-ring except you think not so much good to reward some noble man, then give them the-ring for that dignified people honourable that accept.	But I wish to advise you", he said, "that you do not give the ring to anyone, unless you think it will be good to reward some noble man, then give them the ring, for dignified and honourable people will accept.

The Tale of Auðun of the West Fjords (Old Icelandic)

Old Icelandic	Literal	English
Og far nú heill".	And travel now whole".	And now travel whole".

4

Síðan lætur hann í haf og kemur í Noreg og lætur flytja upp varnað sinn og þurfti nú meira við það en fyrr er hann var í Noregi.	Afterwards laid he to sea and came to Norway and had carried up wares his and needed now more with that than before when he was in Norway.	Afterwards he put to sea and came to Norway and had his wares carried up, which he needed more now than before, when he was in Norway.
Hann fer nú síðan á fund Haralds konungs og vill efna það er hann hét honum áður hann fór til Danmerkur og kveður konung vel.	He travelled now afterwards to meet Harald the-king and wished carry-out that which he promised him before he travelled to Denmark and greeted the-king well.	He travelled now afterwards to meet King Harald, as he wished to carry out what he had promised him, before he travelled to Denmark, and he greeted the king well.
Haraldur konungur tók vel kveðju hans "og sest niður", segir hann, "og drekk hér með oss".	Harald the-king received well greeting his "and sit down" said he, "and drink here with us".	King Harald received his greeting well, "and sit down", he said, "and drink here with us".
Og svo gerir hann.	And so did he.	And so he did.
Þá spurði Haraldur konungur:	Then asked Harald the-king:	Then King Harald asked:
"Hverju launaði Sveinn konungur þér dýrið?"	"How rewarded Svein the-king you the-beast?"	"How did King Svein reward you for the beast?".
Auðun svarar:	Audun answered:	Audun answered:
"Því herra að hann þá að mér".	"Because lord that he then at me".	"Because lord, that he accepted it of me".
Konungur sagði:	The-king said:	The king said:
"Launað mundi eg þér því hafa. Hverju launaði hann enn?"	"Repaid should i you accordingly have. How rewarded he then?"	"I would have repaid you accordingly. How did he reward you then?".
Auðun svarar:	Audun answered:	Audun answered:
"Gaf hann mér silfur til suðurgöngu".	"Gave he me silver to south-going".	"He gave me silver to go south".
Þá segir Haraldur konungur:	Then said Harald the-king:	Then King Harald said:

The Tale of Auðun of the West Fjords (Old Icelandic)

Old Icelandic	Literal	English
"Mörgum manni gefur Sveinn konungur silfur til suðurgöngu eða annarra hluta þótt ekki færi honum gersemar.	"Many people gives Svein the-king silver to south-going or others lots though not bring him treasure.	"King Svein gives many people silver to go south, lots of others, though they do not bring him treasure".
Hvað er enn fleira?"	What was it more?"	What was it more?".
"Hann bauð mér", segir Auðun, "að gerast skutilsveinn hans og mikinn sóma til mín að leggja".	"He bid me" said Audun, "to be cup-bearer his and much honour to me that granted".	"He invited me", said Audun, "to be his cup-bearer and to grant me much honour".
"Vel var það mælt", segir konungur, "og launa mundi hann enn fleira".	"Well was that said" said the-king, "and rewarded would he then more".	"That was well said", said the king, "and he would reward you more".
Auðun segir:	Audun said:	Audun said:
"Gaf hann mér knörr með farmi þeim er hingað er best varið í Noreg".	"Gave he me a-ship with cargo then that there was best wares in Norway".	"He then gave me a ship with cargo, of wares that sell best in Norway".
"Það var stórmannlegt", segir konungur, "en launað mundi eg þér því hafa. Launaði hann því fleira?"	"That was great-man-like" said the-king, "but rewarded would i you accordingly have. Rewarded he then more?"	"That was generous", said the king, "but I would have rewarded you accordingly. Did he reward you then more?".
Auðun segir:	Audun said:	Audun said:
"Gaf hann mér leðurhosu fulla af silfri og kvað mig þá eigi félausan ef eg héldi því þó að skip mitt bryti við Ísland".	"Gave he to-me leather-purse full of silver and said to-me then not money-less if i held therefore though that ship mine break at Iceland".	"He gave me a leather purse full of silver, and said to me that if I held it I would therefore not be penniless, even if my ship was wrecked in Iceland".
Konungur segir:	The-king said:	The king said:
"Það var ágætlega gert og það mundi eg ekki gert hafa. Laus mundi eg þykjast ef eg gæfi þér skipið. Hvort launaði hann fleira?"	"That was greatly done and that would i not done have. Less should i seem if i gave you the-ship. How rewarded he more?"	"That was greatly done, and I would not have done that. Less would I think, if I gave you the ship. How did he reward you more?".

The Tale of Auðun of the West Fjords (Old Icelandic)

Old Icelandic	Literal	English
"Svo var víst herra", segir Auðun, "að hann launaði. Hann gaf mér hring þenna er eg hefi á hendi og kvað svo mega að berast að eg týndi fénu öllu og sagði mig þá eigi félausan ef eg ætti hringinn og bað mig eigi lóga nema eg ætti nakkverjum tignum manni svo gott að launa að eg vildi gefa.	"So was certainly lord" said Audun, "that he rewarded. He gave me ring this that i have in hand and said so may it bear that i lose money all and said to-me then not money-less if i had the-ring and bid me not lose except i have some noble man so good to repay that i wish give.	"So it certainly was, lord", said Audun, "that he rewarded. He gave me this ring, that I have in hand, and so it may bear, though I lose all my money, it is said to me that I would not be penniless, if I had the ring, and he asked me not to part with it, unless I have some noble man so good to repay, that I wish to give it to.
En nú hefi eg þann fundið því að þú áttir kost að taka hvorttveggja frá mér, dýrið og svo líf mitt, en þú lést mig fara þangað í friði sem aðrir náðu eigi".	But now have i then found because that you have benefit to take either-way from me, the-beast and so life mine, but you let me travel from-here in peace as others reached not".	But now then I have found, because you could have taken away from me, the beast or my life, but you let me travel from here in peace, as others could not".
Konungur tók við gjöfinni með blíði og gaf Auðuni í móti góðar gjafar áður en þeir skildust.	The-king received with the-gift with joyfulness and gave Audun in return good gifts before that they separated.	The king received the gift with joyfulness and gave Audun good gifts in return, before they separated.
Auðun varði fénu til Íslandsferðar og fór út þegar um sumarið til Íslands og þótti vera hinn mesti gæfumaður.	Audun was wealth to Iceland-journey and travelled out from-there about summer to Iceland and thought was the most gifted-man.	Audun used his wealth to travel to Iceland and travelled out from there around summer to Iceland and he was thought of as the most gifted man.
Frá þessum manni, Auðuni, var kominn Þorsteinn Gyðuson.	From this people, Audun, was descended Thorstein Gyduson.	From these people, Audun, were descended Thorstein Gyduson.

Word List *(Old Icelandic to English)*

Old Icelandic	English

A, a

að	about, at, by, it, that, to
aðrir	others
af	from, of, off, out-of
aftaninn	evening
aftur	back, returning
albúið	all-prepared
aldregi	never
alla	all
allan	all
allri	all
allt	all
annarra	others
Auðun	Audun (name)
Auðunar	Audun (name)
Auðuni	Audun (name)
augsýn	eyesight
austur	east
Austurveg	Eastern-lands (place)

Á, á

á	a, about, an, and, be, for, in, it, of, on, that, the, to
áður	after, before
ágætlega	greatly
Áka	Aki (name)
ákaflega	extremely
Áki	Aki (name)
álengdar	all-longer
ármaðurinn	steward
ármanni	the-steward
ármanns	steward
átti	had
áttir	have
áttu	have-you

Æ, æ

ætla	intend
ætlað	intended
ætlaði	intended
ætlar	intend, intended
ætti	had, have

B, b

bað	asked, bid
báðir	both
bæði	asked, both
bauð	bid
berast	bear
best	best
betur	better
biðja	begging
biður	asked
bjarndýr	bear
bjarndýri	a-bear, bear
bjarndýrið	the-bear
björg	aid, help
blíði	joyfulness
borðinu	table
brátt	soon
braut	away
brjótir	wrecked
brott	away
bryggjur	quay
bryti	break
brýtur	wrecked
bú	a-farm
búa	prepared
búanda	farmer
búast	prepared
búið	settled
búna	prepared
býður	bid

Word List (Old Icelandic to English)

Old Icelandic	English

D, d

dag	day
Danmerkur	Denmark (place)
Danmörk	Denmark (place)
deyja	die
drekk	drink
drepinn	killed
dró	drew
drukknir	in-drink
drykkju	drinking
dvalist	dwelled
dýr	wild-animal
dýrið	a-beast, animal, beast, the-beast
dýrsins	the-beast

E, e

eða	or
ef	if
efna	carry-out
eftir	after, afterwards, behind
eg	i
ei	not
eiga	not, own, owned
eigi	none, not
eign	owned
eigu	own, owned
einhverju	one-such
einn	one
einu	one
eitt	one
eitthvert	some-kind
ekki	not
em	am
en	and, but, than, that, then
enn	it, one, then
er	as, i, is, that, the, was, what, when, which, who
ert	are
ertu	are-you
eru	they-are, were

F, f

fá	get, give
færa	bring
færð	go
færi	bring, travelled
færir	travel
fagurlega	beautifully
fannst	found
far	travel
fara	travel, travelled
farið	fared, gone
farir	travel
farmi	cargo
fé	money
féið	treasure
félaus	money-less
félausan	money-less
félítill	fee-little
féll	fell
fénu	cargo, money, wealth
fer	travelled
ferð	travel
ferðar	journey
ferðarinnar	travelling
ferst	travelled
finna	found, to-meet
fjár	wealth
fjárins	of-wealth
fjörðum	fields
fleira	more
flytja	carried
fögru	beautiful
fór	travelled
fóta	feet
frá	from
fram	forth, from
frama	confidence
friði	peace
fulla	full
fund	meet
fundar	meet
fundið	found, met

Word List (Old Icelandic to English)

Old Icelandic	English
fyrir	because, before, for, present
fyrr	before, for
fýsir	desire
fýsist	desire

G, g

Old Icelandic	English
gæfi	gave
gæfumaður	gifted-man
gaf	gave, have
gafst	gave
ganga	going, to-go
gangi	come
gef	give
gefa	give
gefi	give
gefið	gave, given
gefir	gave, give
gefur	gives
gekk	going, went
gengi	went
gengu	went
gengur	went
gera	did, do, made, make
gerast	be
gerðist	did
gerir	did, made
gersemar	treasure
gersemi	treasure, treasured
gert	done
getið	told-of
giftu	give
giftumaður	gifted-man
gjafar	gifts
gjöfina	the-gift
gjöfinni	the-gift
góða	good
góðar	good
góðs	good
göfgum	noble
gott	good
Grænlandi	Greenland (place)
Grænlands	Greenland (place)
grunar	suspect

Old Icelandic	English
Guð	God (name)
gull	gold
Gyðuson	Gyduson (name)

H, h

Old Icelandic	English
hætt	at-risk
haf	sea
hafa	have
hafði	had
hafi	have
hafir	have
hafna	harbour
haldið	holding
hálft	half
handar	hand
hann	he, he himself, him
hans	him, his
Haraldi	Harald (name)
Haralds	Harald (name)
Haraldur	Harald (name)
héðan	from-here, hence
hefi	have
hefir	had, has, have
hefta	stop
heill	whole
heiti	promise
héldi	held
heldur	hold, rather
hendi	hand
hér	here
herbergi	a-room
herra	lord
hét	named, promised
heyrt	heard
hingað	there
hinn	the
hirðin	courtiers, the-courtiers
hirðina	guardsmen
hirðmennirnir	the-courtiers
hitt	find
hitta	meet
hlæja	laugh
hlógu	laughed

Word List (Old Icelandic to English)

Old Icelandic	English
hluta	lot, lots
hluturinn	thing
höfum	have
höllina	the-hall
hönd	hand
honum	he, him, to-him
hríð	awhile
hring	a-ring, ring
hringinn	the-ring
hringinum	the-ring
hvað	what
hve	how
hver	every, who
hverju	how
hversu	how-so
hví	why
hvort	how, whether
hvorttveggja	either-way
hygg	think

I, i

illa	ill
illt	ill
inn	inside

Í, í

í	a, for, in, is, it, of, on, to
íhugaði	considered
Ísland	Iceland (place)
Íslandi	Iceland (place)
Íslands	Iceland (place)
íslandsferðar	Iceland-journey
Íslenskur	Icelander (name)

J, j

játum	profess
jók	increased

K, k

Old Icelandic	English
kæmi	came
kæmist	comes
kann	can
kastað	cast
kaupir	bought
kemst	came
kemur	came
kenndi	knew, recognised
keypti	purchased
keyptir	bought
kirkju	church
kirkjuskoti	church-wing
klæði	clothes
klakklaust	unhurt
knörr	a-ship
kollóttur	bald
kom	came, come
koma	came, come
komast	come
komið	come
kominn	coming, descended
komist	coming
konung	the-king
konungi	the-king, the-king's
konunginn	the-king
konungs	the-king
konungur	the-king
kosið	choice
kost	benefit
kunnustu	knew-how
kvað	said
kveðið	said
kveðju	greeting
kveðst	said
kveður	greeted
kveldið	evening
kveldsöngs	evensong
kyni	kin

L, l

lætur	had, laid

Word List (Old Icelandic to English)

Old Icelandic	English
lagði	enriched, laid
land	land
landa	land, lands
landi	land
landið	land
landinu	this-land
láta	let
laug	bath
laun	reward
launa	repay, reward, rewarded
launað	repaid, rewarded
launaði	rewarded
launar	repays
laus	less
leðurhosu	leather-purse
leggja	grant, granted
leið	journey, passed
leiðar	the-way
leiðir	led, took
leigir	rented
lést	let, said
lét	had
letja	discourage
liðu	passed
líf	life
liggja	lay-out
líst	appears
líta	look
lítt	little
lítur	looked
lóga	lose
lokið	ended

M, m

Old Icelandic	English
má	may
maður	a-man, man
maðurinn	a-man
mælt	said, spoken
mælti	spoke
Mæri	Moer (place)
mætti	might
magran	thin
maklegt	proper

Old Icelandic	English
mann	a-man, man
manni	man, people
mannlega	man-like
margir	many
mataðist	ate
matar	food
máttu	might
með	along, with
meðan	while
mega	may
meira	more
menn	people
mér	me, to-me
mestan	most
mesti	most
meta	value
mig	i, me, to-me
mikið	great, much
mikil	much
mikinn	a-great, much
mikla	much
miklar	much
miklu	much
milli	between
mín	me, mine
minni	mine
mislíka	mislike
mitt	mine
mjög	much
móðir	mother
móður	mother
mönnum	people
mörgum	many
móti	meeting, return
mun	could, shall, should
mundi	should, would
mundu	would
muni	shall
munir	should
muntu	shall-you

N, n

Old Icelandic	English
náðu	reached
nakkvarra	some

Word List (Old Icelandic to English)

Old Icelandic	English
nakkverjar	some
nakkverjum	some
nauðsyn	necessary
nema	except
niður	down
nokkuð	sometime
Noreg	Norway (place)
Noregi	Norway (place)
Noregs	Norway (place)
nú	not, now
nýtur	benefit

O, o

of	of, over, to
ofan	over-to
og	also, and
orðið	become
oss	us

Ó, ó

ófrið	un-peace
ósællegur	unhappy
óvinur	un-friend
óvitur	unwise

Ö, ö

öðru	other
öllu	all
öngu	none
öræfi	wild

P, p

páskum	easter
peningur	penny

R, r

Old Icelandic	English
ráð	course
ráða	advise
ráði	decided
reiðfara	voyage
réttara	righter
Rómaborg	Rome-city (place)
rúmferla	rome-travellers
rúmferlum	rome-travellers

S, s

sá	saw, so
sættast	reconciled
sagði	said, said
sagt	said, told
sál	soul
saman	the-same
sannlegt	true-like
satt	true
sáumst	saw
Saxland	Saxon-lands (place)
sé	is
séð	seen
seg	say
segir	said, says, told
seint	coldly
seldi	handed-over
selja	sell
selur	sell
sem	as, since, such, that, what
sendir	sent
sér	he, him, himself, his, themselves, to-you, yourself
sért	yourself
sest	sit
setti	intended
síðan	after, afterwards, since, then
siður	custom
sig	himself
silfri	silver
silfur	silver
sín	him

Word List (Old Icelandic to English)

Old Icelandic	English
sína	his
sinn	his
sinnar	his
sinni	he, his, on-the-way
sitt	his
sjá	seen, so
skal	shall
skaltu	shall
skapi	mind
skildust	separated
skip	ship, ships, the-ship
skipaði	directed
skipast	changed
skipi	ship, the-ship
skipið	ship, the-ship
skipinu	the-ship
skipsbrotum	ship-wreck
skipum	ships
skreppu	pouch
skulu	shall
skutilsvein	cup-bearer
skutilsveinn	cup-bearer
slík	such
slíka	such
slíku	such
sóma	honour
sómir	honourable
sótt	sickness
spurði	asked
spurt	heard
staddur	standing
staf	staff
stafkarls	beggar's-path, the-beggar's
starfaði	worked
stíg	path
stigi	climbed
stóðu	stood
stórmannlegt	great-man-like
stund	awhile
stundir	time
stýrimanni	skipper
stýrimanns	skipper
suður	south
suðurgöngu	south-going
sumarið	summer
svarar	answered
Svein	Svein (name)
Sveini	Svein (name)
Sveinn	Svein (name)
Sveins	Svein (name), Svein's (name)
Svíþjóðar	Sweden (place)
svo	so, such
sýnist	considered, seems

T, t

Old Icelandic	English
taka	take
tálma	prevent
tekur	taking, took
tíðir	a-time
tignum	dignified, noble
til	for, to, until
tók	received, took
troði	treads
tvö	twice
týndi	lose
týnir	lose

Þ, þ

Old Icelandic	English
þá	then
það	it, that
þakkaði	thanked
þakki	thank
þangað	from-here, there
þann	then, this
þar	then, there
þars	there
þegar	as-soon-as, from-there, straight-away
þegið	received
þeim	them, then, they
þeir	there, they
þeirri	there
þekkist	knew
þekkti	noticed
þenna	this
þér	to-you, you, your

Word List (Old Icelandic to English)

Old Icelandic	English
þess	this
þessa	this
þessi	this
þessu	this
þessum	this
þetta	this
þið	you
þig	you
þiggja	accept
þína	you, yours
þinnar	your
þó	though
þökk	thanks
þorði	dared
Þóri	Thorir (name)
Þóris	Thorir (name)
Þorsteini	Thorstein (name)
Þorsteinn	Thorstein (name)
Þorsteins	Thorstein (name)
þótt	though
þótti	thought
þóttist	thought
þriggja	three
þú	you
þurfið	need
þurfti	needed
því	accordingly, because, for, then, therefore
þykist	think
þykja	think
þykjast	seem

U, u

um	about, around
umráði	managed
umsjá	about-see
undarlega	strange
uns	until
upp	up
uppi	up
utan	out
utanferðina	out-travelling

Ú, ú

úr	out-of
út	out
úti	outside

V, v

væri	should-be
værir	would-be
valdi	will
var	as, was
varði	was
varið	wares
varla	hardly
varnað	wares
veik	turned-to
veit	knew
vel	well
velkominn	well
ver	be
vér	we
vera	be, was
verð	worth
verða	be, become, was
verði	be, worth
verður	was
Vestfirskur	Westfjords (place)
vestur	west
vetra	winters
veturinn	winter
við	at, we, with
víða	widely
Vík	Vik (place)
vil	will, wish
vildi	wish, wished
vildir	wish
viljið	wish
vill	wished, wishes
vilt	wish
viltu	will, will-you
virðing	worth
vist	hospitality
víst	certainly

Word List (Old Icelandic to English)

Old Icelandic	English
vista	provisions
vistir	provisions
vita	know
vor	our
vorið	spring
voru	were

Y, y

yðru	your, yours
yður	you, your

Ý, ý

ýmissa	various

Word List *(English to Old Icelandic)*

English	Old Icelandic

A, a

English	Old Icelandic
a	*á, í*
a-bear	*bjarndýri*
a-beast	*dýrið*
about	*á, að, um*
about-see	*umsjá*
accept	*þiggja*
accordingly	*því*
advise	*ráða*
a-farm	*bú*
after	*áður, eftir, síðan*
afterwards	*eftir, síðan*
a-great	*mikinn*
aid	*björg*
Aki (name)	*Áka, Áki*
all	*alla, allan, allri, allt, öllu*
all-longer	*álengdar*
all-prepared	*albúið*
along	*með*
also	*og*
am	*em*
a-man	*maður, maðurinn, mann*
an	*á*
and	*á, en, og*
animal	*dýrið*
answered	*svarar*
appears	*líst*
are	*ert*
are-you	*ertu*
a-ring	*hring*
a-room	*herbergi*
around	*um*
as	*er, sem, var*
a-ship	*knörr*
asked	*bað, bæði, biður, spurði*
as-soon-as	*þegar*
at	*að, við*
ate	*mataðist*
a-time	*tíðir*
at-risk	*hætt*
Audun (name)	*Auðun, Auðunar, Auðuni*
away	*braut, brott*
awhile	*hríð, stund*

B, b

English	Old Icelandic
back	*aftur*
bald	*kollóttur*
bath	*laug*
be	*á, gerast, ver, vera, verða, verði*
bear	*berast, bjarndýr, bjarndýri*
beast	*dýrið*
beautiful	*fögru*
beautifully	*fagurlega*
because	*fyrir, því*
become	*orðið, verða*
before	*áður, fyrir, fyrr*
beggar's-path	*stafkarls*
begging	*biðja*
behind	*eftir*
benefit	*kost, nýtur*
best	*best*
better	*betur*
between	*milli*
bid	*bað, bauð, býður*
both	*báðir, bæði*
bought	*kaupir, keyptir*
break	*bryti*
bring	*færa, færi*
but	*en*
by	*að*

C, c

English	Old Icelandic
came	*kæmi, kemst, kemur, kom, koma*
can	*kann*

Word List (English to Old Icelandic)

English	*Old Icelandic*	English	*Old Icelandic*
cargo	*farmi, fénu*		
carried	*flytja*		
carry-out	*efna*	**E, e**	
cast	*kastað*		
certainly	*víst*	east	*austur*
changed	*skipast*	easter	*páskum*
choice	*kosið*	Eastern-lands (place)	*Austurveg*
church	*kirkju*	either-way	*hvorttveggja*
church-wing	*kirkjuskoti*	ended	*lokið*
climbed	*stigi*	enriched	*lagði*
clothes	*klæði*	evening	*aftaninn, kveldið*
coldly	*seint*	evensong	*kveldsöngs*
come	*gangi, kom, koma, komast, komið*	every	*hver*
		except	*nema*
comes	*kæmist*	extremely	*ákaflega*
coming	*kominn, komist*	eyesight	*augsýn*
confidence	*frama*		
considered	*íhugaði, sýnist*	**F, f**	
could	*mun*		
course	*ráð*	fared	*farið*
courtiers	*hirðin*	farmer	*búanda*
cup-bearer	*skutilsvein, skutilsveinn*	fee-little	*félítill*
		feet	*fóta*
custom	*siður*	fell	*féll*
		fields	*fjörðum*
D, d		find	*hitt*
		food	*matar*
dared	*þorði*	for	*á, fyrir, fyrr, í, því, til*
day	*dag*	forth	*fram*
decided	*ráði*	found	*fannst, finna, fundið*
Denmark (place)	*Danmerkur, Danmörk*	from	*af, frá, fram*
descended	*kominn*	from-here	*héðan, þangað*
desire	*fýsir, fýsist*	from-there	*þegar*
did	*gera, gerðist, gerir*	full	*fulla*
die	*deyja*		
dignified	*tignum*	**G, g**	
directed	*skipaði*		
discourage	*letja*	gave	*gæfi, gaf, gafst, gefið, gefir*
do	*gera*		
done	*gert*	get	*fá*
down	*niður*	gifted-man	*gæfumaður, giftumaður*
drew	*dró*		
drink	*drekk*	gifts	*gjafar*
drinking	*drykkju*	give	*fá, gef, gefa, gefi, gefir, giftu*
dwelled	*dvalist*		

Word List (English to Old Icelandic)

English	Old Icelandic
given	*gefið*
gives	*gefur*
go	*færð*
God (name)	*Guð*
going	*ganga, gekk*
gold	*gull*
gone	*farið*
good	*góða, góðar, góðs, gott*
grant	*leggja*
granted	*leggja*
great	*mikið*
greatly	*ágætlega*
great-man-like	*stórmannlegt*
Greenland (place)	*Grænlandi, Grænlands*
greeted	*kveður*
greeting	*kveðju*
guardsmen	*hirðina*
Gyduson (name)	*Gyðuson*

H, h

English	Old Icelandic
had	*ætti, átti, hafði, hefir, lætur, lét*
half	*hálft*
hand	*handar, hendi, hönd*
handed-over	*seldi*
Harald (name)	*Haraldi, Haralds, Haraldur*
harbour	*hafna*
hardly	*varla*
has	*hefir*
have	*ætti, áttir, gaf, hafa, hafi, hafir, hefi, hefir, höfum*
have-you	*áttu*
he	*hann, honum, sér, sinni*
he himself	*hann*
heard	*heyrt, spurt*
held	*héldi*
help	*björg*
hence	*héðan*
here	*hér*
him	*hann, hans, honum, sér, sín*
himself	*sér, sig*
his	*hans, sér, sína, sinn, sinnar, sinni, sitt*
hold	*heldur*
holding	*haldið*
honour	*sóma*
honourable	*sómir*
hospitality	*vist*
how	*hve, hverju, hvort*
how-so	*hversu*

I, i

English	Old Icelandic
i	*eg, er, mig*
Iceland (place)	*Ísland, Íslandi, Íslands*
Icelander (name)	*Íslenskur*
Iceland-journey	*íslandsferðar*
if	*ef*
ill	*illa, illt*
in	*á, í*
increased	*jók*
in-drink	*drukknir*
inside	*inn*
intend	*ætla, ætlar*
intended	*ætlað, ætlaði, ætlar, setti*
is	*er, í, sé*
it	*á, að, enn, í, það*

J, j

English	Old Icelandic
journey	*ferðar, leið*
joyfulness	*blíði*

K, k

English	Old Icelandic
killed	*drepinn*
kin	*kyni*
knew	*kenndi, þekkist, veit*
knew-how	*kunnustu*
know	*vita*

Word List (English to Old Icelandic)

English	*Old Icelandic*

L, l

laid	*lætur, lagði*
land	*land, landa, landi, landið*
lands	*landa*
laugh	*hlæja*
laughed	*hlógu*
lay-out	*liggja*
leather-purse	*leðurhosu*
led	*leiðir*
less	*laus*
let	*láta, lést*
life	*líf*
little	*lítt*
look	*líta*
looked	*lítur*
lord	*herra*
lose	*lóga, týndi, týnir*
lot	*hluta*
lots	*hluta*

M, m

made	*gera, gerir*
make	*gera*
man	*maður, mann, manni*
managed	*umráði*
man-like	*mannlega*
many	*margir, mörgum*
may	*má, mega*
me	*mér, mig, mín*
meet	*fund, fundar, hitta*
meeting	*móti*
met	*fundið*
might	*mætti, máttu*
mind	*skapi*
mine	*mín, minni, mitt*
mislike	*mislíka*
Moer (place)	*Mæri*
money	*fé, fénu*
money-less	*félaus, félausan*
more	*fleira, meira*
most	*mestan, mesti*
mother	*móðir, móður*
much	*mikið, mikil, mikinn, mikla, miklar, miklu, mjög*

N, n

named	*hét*
necessary	*nauðsyn*
need	*þurfið*
needed	*þurfti*
never	*aldregi*
noble	*göfgum, tignum*
none	*eigi, öngu*
Norway (place)	*Noreg, Noregi, Noregs*
not	*ei, eiga, eigi, ekki, nú*
noticed	*þekkti*
now	*nú*

O, o

of	*á, af, í, of*
off	*af*
of-wealth	*fjárins*
on	*á, í*
one	*einn, einu, eitt, enn*
one-such	*einhverju*
on-the-way	*sinni*
or	*eða*
other	*öðru*
others	*aðrir, annarra*
our	*vor*
out	*út, utan*
out-of	*af, úr*
outside	*úti*
out-travelling	*utanferðina*
over	*of*
over-to	*ofan*
own	*eiga, eigu*
owned	*eiga, eign, eigu*

P, p

Word List (English to Old Icelandic)

English	*Old Icelandic*	English	*Old Icelandic*
passed	*leið, liðu*	said	*kvað, kveðið, kveðst, lést, mælt, sagði, sagði, sagt, segir*
path	*stíg*		
peace	*friði*		
penny	*peningur*	saw	*sá, sáumst*
people	*manni, menn, mönnum*	Saxon-lands (place)	*Saxland*
		say	*seg*
pouch	*skreppu*	says	*segir*
prepared	*búa, búast, búna*	sea	*haf*
present	*fyrir*	seem	*þykjast*
prevent	*tálma*	seems	*sýnist*
profess	*játum*	seen	*séð, sjá*
promise	*heiti*	sell	*selja, selur*
promised	*hét*	sent	*sendir*
proper	*maklegt*	separated	*skildust*
provisions	*vista, vistir*	settled	*búið*
purchased	*keypti*	shall	*mun, muni, skal, skaltu, skulu*

Q, q

		shall-you	*muntu*
quay	*bryggjur*	ship	*skip, skipi, skipið*
		ships	*skip, skipum*
		ship-wreck	*skipsbrotum*

R, r

		should	*mun, mundi, munir*
		should-be	*væri*
		sickness	*sótt*
rather	*heldur*	silver	*silfri, silfur*
reached	*náðu*	since	*sem, síðan*
received	*þegið, tók*	sit	*sest*
recognised	*kenndi*	skipper	*stýrimanni, stýrimanns*
reconciled	*sættast*		
rented	*leigir*	so	*sá, sjá, svo*
repaid	*launað*	some	*nakkvarra, nakkverjar, nakkverjum*
repay	*launa*		
repays	*launar*	some-kind	*eitthvert*
return	*móti*	sometime	*nokkuð*
returning	*aftur*	soon	*brátt*
reward	*laun, launa*	soul	*sál*
rewarded	*launa, launað, launaði*	south	*suður*
		south-going	*suðurgöngu*
righter	*réttara*	spoke	*mælti*
ring	*hring*	spoken	*mælt*
Rome-city (place)	*Rómaborg*	spring	*vorið*
rome-travellers	*rúmferla, rúmferlum*	staff	*staf*
		standing	*staddur*
		steward	*ármaðurinn, ármanns*

S, s

		stood	*stóðu*

Word List (English to Old Icelandic)

English	*Old Icelandic*
stop	*hefta*
straight-away	*þegar*
strange	*undarlega*
such	*sem, slík, slíka, slíku, svo*
summer	*sumarið*
suspect	*grunar*
Svein (name)	*Svein, Sveini, Sveinn, Sveins*
Svein's (name)	*Sveins*
Sweden (place)	*Svíþjóðar*

T, t

English	*Old Icelandic*
table	*borðinu*
take	*taka*
taking	*tekur*
than	*en*
thank	*þakki*
thanked	*þakkaði*
thanks	*þökk*
that	*á, að, en, er, sem, það*
the	*á, er, hinn*
the-bear	*bjarndýrið*
the-beast	*dýrið, dýrsins*
the-beggar's	*stafkarls*
the-courtiers	*hirðin, hirðmennirnir*
the-gift	*gjöfina, gjöfinni*
the-hall	*höllina*
the-king	*konung, konungi, konunginn, konungs, konungur*
the-king's	*konungi*
them	*þeim*
themselves	*sér*
then	*en, enn, síðan, þá, þann, þar, þeim, því*
there	*hingað, þangað, þar, þars, þeir, þeirri*
therefore	*því*
the-ring	*hringinn, hringinum*
the-same	*saman*
the-ship	*skip, skipi, skipið, skipinu*
the-steward	*ármanni*

English	*Old Icelandic*
the-way	*leiðar*
they	*þeim, þeir*
they-are	*eru*
thin	*magran*
thing	*hluturinn*
think	*hygg, þykist, þykja*
this	*þann, þenna, þess, þessa, þessi, þessu, þessum, þetta*
this-land	*landinu*
Thorir (name)	*Þóri, Þóris*
Thorstein (name)	*Þorsteini, Þorsteinn, Þorsteins*
though	*þó, þótt*
thought	*þótti, þóttist*
three	*þriggja*
time	*stundir*
to	*á, að, í, of, til*
to-go	*ganga*
to-him	*honum*
told	*sagt, segir*
told-of	*getið*
to-me	*mér, mig*
to-meet	*finna*
took	*leiðir, tekur, tók*
to-you	*sér, þér*
travel	*færir, far, fara, farir, ferð*
travelled	*færi, fara, fer, ferst, fór*
travelling	*ferðarinnar*
treads	*troði*
treasure	*féið, gersemar, gersemi*
treasured	*gersemi*
true	
true-like	*sannlegt*
turned-to	*veik*
twice	*tvö*

U, u

English	*Old Icelandic*
un-friend	*óvinur*
unhappy	*ósællegur*
unhurt	*klakklaust*
un-peace	*ófrið*

Word List (English to Old Icelandic)

English	*Old Icelandic*
until	*til, uns*
unwise	*óvitur*
up	*upp, uppi*
us	*oss*

V, v

English	*Old Icelandic*
value	*meta*
various	*ýmissa*
Vik (place)	*Vík*
voyage	*reiðfara*

W, w

English	*Old Icelandic*
wares	*varið, varnað*
was	*er, var, varði, vera, verða, verður*
we	*vér, við*
wealth	*fénu, fjár*
well	*vel, velkominn*
went	*gekk, gengi, gengu, gengur*
were	*eru, voru*
west	*vestur*
Westfjords (place)	*Vestfirskur*
what	*er, hvað, sem*
when	*er*
whether	*hvort*
which	*er*
while	*meðan*
who	*er, hver*
whole	*heill*
why	*hví*
widely	*víða*
wild	*öræfi*
wild-animal	*dýr*
will	*valdi, vil, viltu*
will-you	*viltu*
winter	*veturinn*
winters	*vetra*
wish	*vil, vildi, vildir, viljið, vilt*
wished	*vildi, vill*
wishes	*vill*

English	*Old Icelandic*
with	*með, við*
worked	*starfaði*
worth	*verð, verði, virðing*
would	*mundi, mundu*
would-be	*værir*
wrecked	*brjótir, brýtur*

Y, y

English	*Old Icelandic*
you	*þér, þið, þig, þína, þú, yður*
your	*þér, þinnar, yðru, yður*
yours	*þína, yðru*
yourself	*sér, sért*

A Word Comparison of Old Norse and Old Icelandic Words

Old Norse	Old Icelandic	English
áðr	áður	after
áðr	áður	before
ætlaðak	ætlaði	intended
ætlat	ætlað	intended
ætta	ætti	had
ætta	ætti	have
aftr	aftur	back
aftr	aftur	returning
ágætliga	ágætlega	greatly
ákafliga	ákaflega	extremely
albúit	albúið	all-prepared
aldrigi	aldregi	never
álengðar	álengdar	all-longer
ármaðrinn	ármaðurinn	steward
at	að	about
at	að	at
at	að	by
at	að	it
at	að	that
at	að	to
Auðunn	Auðun	Audun (name)
austr	austur	east
Austrveg	Austurveg	Eastern-lands (place)
betr	betur	better
bezt	best	best
biðr	biður	asked
bjarndýrit	bjarndýrið	the-bear
blíðu	blíði	joyfulness
brýtr	brýtur	wrecked
búit	búið	settled
býðr	býður	bid
Danmerkr	Danmerkur	Denmark (place)
dvalizt	dvalist	dwelled
dýrit	dýrið	a-beast
dýrit	dýrið	animal
dýrit	dýrið	beast

Old Norse	Old Icelandic	English
dýrit	dýrið	the-beast
eigi	ei	not
ek	eg	i
engu	öngu	none
fær	færð	go
færa	færi	travelled
fagrliga	fagurlega	beautifully
fannt	fannst	found
farit	farið	fared
farit	farið	gone
féit	féið	treasure
félauss	félaus	money-less
fell	féll	fell
ferr	fer	travelled
ferr	ferð	travel
fundit	fundið	found
fundit	fundið	met
fyr	fyrir	before
fyr	fyrir	for
gæfa	gæfi	gave
gæfumaðr	gæfumaður	gifted-man
gaft	gafst	gave
gefa	gefi	give
gefit	gefið	gave
gefit	gefið	given
gefr	gefur	gives
gengr	gengur	went
gersimar	gersemar	treasure
gersimi	gersemi	treasure
gersimi	gersemi	treasured
getit	getið	told-of
giftumaðr	giftumaður	gifted-man
hafa	hafi	have
haldit	haldið	holding
Haraldr	Haraldur	Harald (name)
héðan	héðan	from-here
héðan	héðan	hence
heit	heiti	promise

A Word Comparison of Old Norse and Old Icelandic Words

Old Norse	Old Icelandic	English
helda	héldi	held
heldr	heldur	hold
heldr	heldur	rather
hingat	hingað	there
hirðmenninir	hirðmennirnir	the-courtiers
hlutrinn	hluturinn	thing
hvárt	hvort	how
hvárt	hvort	whether
hvárttveggja	hvorttveggja	either-way
hvat	hvað	what
hvé	hve	how
hverr	hver	every
hverr	hver	who
inn	hinn	the
Íslenzkr	Íslenskur	Icelander (name)
kastat	kastað	cast
kemr	kemur	came
keyptak	keypti	purchased
klaklaust	klakklaust	unhurt
kollóttr	kollóttur	bald
komit	komið	come
komizt	komist	coming
konungr	konungur	the-king
kosit	kosið	choice
kveðit	kveðið	said
kveðr	kveður	greeted
kveldit	kveldið	evening
lætr	lætur	had
lætr	lætur	laid
lagða	lagði	enriched
landit	landið	land
launat	launað	repaid
launat	launað	rewarded
lauss	laus	less
leðrhosu	leðurhosu	leather-purse
lézt	lést	let
lézt	lést	said
lítr	lítur	looked
lízt	líst	appears
lokit	lokið	ended
maðr	maður	a-man
maðr	maður	man
maðrinn	maðurinn	a-man
mætta	mætti	might
makligt	maklegt	proper
mannliga	mannlega	man-like
mik	mig	i
mik	mig	me
mik	mig	to-me
mikit	mikið	great
mikit	mikið	much
mjök	mjög	much
mynda	mundi	should
mynda	mundi	would
myndi	mundi	should
myndi	mundi	would
niðr	niður	down
nökkurar	nakkverjar	some
nökkurra	nakkvarra	some
nökkurum	nakkverjum	some
nökkut	nokkuð	sometime
Nóreg	Noreg	Norway (place)
Nóregi	Noregi	Norway (place)
Nóregs	Noregs	Norway (place)
nýtr	nýtur	benefit
ok	og	also
ok	og	and
ór	úr	out-of
orðit	orðið	become
ósælligr	ósællegur	unhappy
óvinr	óvinur	un-friend
óvitr	óvitur	unwise
penningr	peningur	penny
sannligt	sannlegt	true-like
segir	svarar	answered
selr	selur	sell
sér	sért	yourself
sét	séð	seen
settak	setti	intended
sezt	sest	sit
siðr	siður	custom
sik	sig	himself
silfr	silfur	silver

A Word Comparison of Old Norse and Old Icelandic Words

Old Norse	Old Icelandic	English	Old Norse	Old Icelandic	English
skilðist	skildust	separated	Vestfirzkr	Vestfirskur	Westfjords (place)
skipazt	skipast	changed	vestr	vestur	west
skipit	skipið	ship	vetrinn	veturinn	winter
skipit	skipið	the-ship	vilda	vildi	wish
staddr	staddur	standing	vilið	viljið	wish
stafkarlsstíg	stafkarls	beggar's-path	vill	vilt	wish
stórmannligt	stórmannlegt	great-man-like	villtu	viltu	will
suðr	suður	south	villtu	viltu	will-you
suðrgöngu	suðurgöngu	south-going	vit	við	we
sumarit	sumarið	summer	yðr	yður	you
svá	svo	so	yðr	yður	your
svá	svo	such			
tekr	tekur	taking			
tekr	tekur	took			
þangat	þangað	from-here			
þangat	þangað	there			
þat	það	it			
þat	það	that			
þegit	þegið	received			
þeiri	þeirri	there			
þekkði	þekkti	noticed			
þik	þig	you			
þit	þið	you			
þurfuð	þurfið	need			
þykkist	þykist	think			
þykkja	þykja	think			
þykkjast	þykjast	seem			
tígnum	tignum	dignified			
tígnum	tignum	noble			
tvau	tvö	twice			
týnda	týndi	lose			
umbráði	umráði	managed			
undarliga	undarlega	strange			
unz	uns	until			
útan	utan	out			
útanferðina	utanferðina	out-travelling			
varit	varið	wares			
várit	vorið	spring			
várr	vor	our			
váru	voru	were			
vel	velkominn	well			
verðr	verður	was			

www.ingramcontent.com/pod-product-compliance
Lightning Source LLC
Chambersburg PA
CBHW051423070526
44584CB00023B/3553